THE
HUMMER
AND THE MINI

NAVIGATING THE CONTRADICTIONS
OF THE NEW TREND LANDSCAPE

Robyn Waters

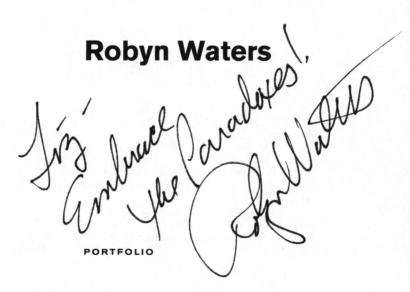

PORTFOLIO

PORTFOLIO
Published by the Penguin Group
Penguin Group (USA) Inc., 375 Hudson Street, New York, New York 10014, U.S.A. ·
Penguin Group (Canada), 90 Eglinton Avenue East , Suite 700, Toronto, Ontario, Canada
M4P 2Y3 (a division of Pearson Penguin Canada Inc.) · Penguin Books Ltd, 80 Strand,
London WC2R 0RL, England · Penguin Ireland, 25 St. Stephen's Green, Dublin 2, Ireland
(a division of Penguin Books Ltd) · Penguin Books Australia Ltd, 250 Camberwell Road,
Camberwell, Victoria 3124, Australia (a division of Pearson Australia Group Pty Ltd) ·
Penguin Books India Pvt Ltd, 11 Community Centre, Panchsheel Park, New Delhi - 110
017, India · Penguin Group (NZ), Cnr Airborne and Rosedale Roads, Albany, Auckland
1310, New Zealand (a division of Pearson New Zealand Ltd) · Penguin Books (South Africa) (Pty) Ltd, 24 Sturdee Avenue, Rosebank, Johannesburg 2196, South Africa

Penguin Books Ltd, Registered Offices:
80 Strand, London WC2R 0RL, England

First published in 2006 by Portfolio,
a member of Penguin Group (USA) Inc.

10 9 8 7 6 5 4 3 2 1

Photograph credits appear on page 223.

Publisher's Note
This publication is designed to provide accurate and authoritative information in regard
to the subject matter covered. It is sold with the understanding that the publisher is not
engaged in rendering legal, accounting or other professional services. If you require legal
advice or other expert assistance, you should seek the services of a competent professional.

LIBRARY OF CONGRESS CATALOGING-IN-PUBLICATION DATA

Waters, Robyn.
    The Hummer and the Mini : navigating the contradictions of the new trend
landscape / Robyn Waters.
        p.   cm.
    Includes index.
    ISBN 1-59184-136-4
    1. Marketing research. 2. New products. 3. Fads. 4. Consumer behavior—Forecasting.
I. Title.
    HF5415.2.W37 2006
    658.8'3—dc22   2006045327

Printed in the United States of America
Set in Minion Display with Berthold Akzidenz Grotesk
Designed by Daniel Lagin

To Gary: A designer who brings beauty to the ordinary.
A cowboy as at home on the range as he is at the opera.
A husband who knows how to hold tight while letting go.

"Serious things cannot be understood without laughable things, nor opposites at all without opposites."

—Plato, 428–348 B.C.

CONTENTS

INTRODUCTION

MY FIRST BOOK, *THE TRENDMASTER'S GUIDE: GET A JUMP on What Your Customer Wants Next,* is a small, witty A-to-Z handbook designed to simplify and demystify the art of trend tracking. It outlines my unique philosophy on tracking and translating trends into sales and profit. It's about the *how* of Trend.

In the last chapter, Z is for Zen, I introduce the reader to my perspective and insights on trend/countertrend. I quote Lao-tzu, ancient Chinese philosopher, who captured the essence of what fascinates me most about the art of trend tracking: "When opposites supplement each other, everything is harmonious." I wrote that "for every yin there is a yang. For every trend there is a countertrend." I encouraged the reader, in true Zen fashion, to "embrace opposites. Celebrate duality. Embrace polarity."

This book picks up where *The Trendmaster's Guide* leaves

off. *The Hummer and the Mini* explores the *what* of Trend. It's an overview of high-level macro trends happening in the world today. In essence, it's a study of paradoxes, concepts that at first glance seem absurd or contradictory, but in reality are absolute truths. Dr. Marty Grothe, in his book *Oxymoronica*, points out that "paradox is a particularly powerful device to ensnare truth because it concisely illuminates the contradictions that are at the very heart of our lives."

Perhaps that's what fascinates me most about paradox; the way it illuminates the truth. A paradox captures the essence of what's going on out there in the world while at the same time cautioning that things aren't always as they appear at first glance. When explored with an open mind, paradoxes will help you read between the lines and reframe your perspective.

Paradoxes are powerful tools that can help you discover the opposing realities of the customer and the contradictory aspects of the marketplace. Too many businesses try to make it a black-and-white proposition. Either/or. I believe that within the paradox lies an opportunity to get out of the black-and-white box and step into a world of colorful possibilities.

My years at Target taught me a thing or two about paradox. When I came to Target in 1992, it was a small regional discounter with a funny bull's-eye logo trying to survive in a marketplace dominated by Wal-Mart and cluttered with many other small regional discounters. Target realized that in order to survive, let alone compete in that retail scene, it would have to "differentiate or die." The discounters that didn't figure that out, did in fact die off . . . Venture, Zayres, to name two. And Kmart is still struggling to keep its head above water.

Target's formula was a simple one, consisting of three parts. First, the company was determined to capitalize on its department store heritage and be the first discounter to be "trend right." Rather than carrying last year's best sellers the following year at a reduced price, our goal was to have the same products on our floors at the same time that Gap, Crate & Barrel, and Banana Republic were stocking, only at better prices.

The second part of the formula was to be "guest focused." We called our customers guests, in the tradition of Disney. We wanted to know not just the age, income level, and zip codes of our customers; we wanted to know what their lives were like, how they lived, what they felt, and what they cared about.

The third part of the formula was the "secret sauce." The company made a huge commitment to design. Design would be the tool used to translate the trends into great products and experiences that made sense for our guests' lives. Ultimately, design was the competitive weapon that brought beauty not just to the product, but to the bottom line. It brought credibility to the brand promise "Expect More. Pay Less." It's also what helped turn Target into *Tarzhay*.

Trend right. Guest focused. Design driven. The three key elements of the strategy that ultimately turned Target into *the upscale discounter*. Now there's a paradox.

The trends outlined in this book are all paradoxes. They highlight the contradictory nature of these trends, and I hope they will help you reevaluate your point of view. The insights I share in this book will take you deep into the hearts and minds of your customer to help you determine not just what's *next*, but what's *important*.

You will find no big pronouncements here. No predictions. No prescriptions. And no pat answers. Charles Handy, a pre-eminent British management guru and one of my business heroes said: "Paradoxes are like the weather; something to be lived with, not solved." Instead of *answers*, I hope to help you discover the *possibilities*. This book will help you explore the apparent contradictions manifesting themselves out there on the treacherous trend landscape. I hope it ultimately provides you a new way of looking at your world.

As I travel the country sharing my philosophy on the art of trend, I've been amazed at how open people really are to looking at things differently. Corporations have finally realized that they can't *cut* their way to greatness anymore. Instead, it's time to put something back *into* the product. That takes real innovation, and innovation usually requires doing things in a new way.

Many of the stories that I profile in the book are examples of businesses that at one time might have thought inside the box when the marketplace was a simpler, more sane place. To-day, however, companies such as Starbucks, Whole Foods, Mini Cooper, M&M's, Costco, Jones Soda, DaVinci Slate, and MetroNaps have all realized that there is no box. It's no longer even a matter of thinking outside the box. Companies that have embraced change and accepted the idea of the contradictory consumer have found delightful ways to reframe their business propositions. By paying attention to both ends of the trend spectrum, they've been able to develop a unique proposition that helps drive their success.

Businesses today need to embrace change and live with the paradoxes. They have to admit to themselves that *the same old, same old* just won't do. I hope this book provides a little guidance, a polite nudge, and some interesting insights to help you not just think outside the box, but to throw the box away altogether.

We live in a world filled with paradox. It's a fact of life. Margaret Mead said, "We should always remember that we are absolutely unique, just like everyone else." If you can embrace that thought, you'll have no problem embracing the paradoxes contained within.

CHAPTER 1
TREND/COUNTERTREND

WHEN I BEGAN MY CAREER IN THE LATE 1970S, THE TREND-
spotting business was pretty black and white. A trend was defined as something that *everyone* wanted at the same time. Fashion magazines and business publications alike regularly proclaimed what was "in" and what was "out." Trends were distilled down to easy-to-decipher "thumbs up" or "thumbs down" messaging.

Back then, if you kept your antennae up, your radar out, and connected the dots, you could pretty much determine what the next big trend was going to be. If you were smart enough to do something about it fairly quickly, you could make a lot of money and ride that trend all the way to the bank.

Sometime during the late nineties it became very trendy, to be trendy and the business of "cool hunting" was born. Cool hunters were those *über*-hip bohemian types who were always on the lookout for the next big thing. Manufacturers paid big bucks to hear their pronouncements. Marketers developed elaborate campaigns to capitalize on their trend predictions. Fashion magazines vied for newsstand sales by leveraging the cool factor and being first with the latest trend info. Cool hunting quickly became the Holy Grail for increased sales.

Then, just when we thought we had it all figured out, everything changed. It was as if overnight the consumer developed a severe case of schizophrenia. Tangible consumer *need* became eclipsed by abstract *desire* as consumers faced an unprecedented array of options. In this changing environment, a cookie-cutter approach to spotting trends no longer sufficed. I had to admit that as a Trendmaster I could no longer deliver the answer to the question What is the next big thing?

The reason was glaringly obvious: There wasn't just one next big thing. Rather, there were many different next big things, and they were happening concurrently. It became clear that for every trend there was a countertrend, and both were equally valid. The trend itself wasn't what was important anymore. It was how the trend meshed with the consumer's conflicted, paradoxical, and often counterintuitive desires that really mattered.

The very idea that there might not be just *one right answer* flew in the face of current corporate philosophy. After all, we had entered the age of Six Sigma. With enough analysis, number crunching, flowcharting, and research you were supposed to be able to come up with a single best method or process—one right answer or way of doing something, period. We could chart and plan our way into the hearts of customers. No ifs, ands, or buts. My problem around this time, though, was that I kept seeing the "buts."

I had begun to realize that there were many different ways to satisfy the same customer. I no longer believed that there was one right way or best method to design a product, merchandise a line, or assort a department. It probably had something to do with the way our lives had been shifting and meshing over time—the way the social fabric of our lives had become complicated and fragmented, and in many ways, paradoxical. You might be a carpooling mom one moment, dynamic career woman the next, or a hard-hitting corporate boss at the Monday-morning meeting and a Little League coach that afternoon. Because people were no longer fitting into just one category—mom, executive, coach—I had to become more flexible in the way I thought about and reached out to consumers.

BREAKING THE RULES

I started seeing the emergence of this paradox around the time Sharon Stone paired a Gap mock turtleneck with an Armani jacket and Valentino skirt and wore it to the Oscars. Up until then, there was a more predictable formula at play. It used to be that the woman who wore a Chanel suit had the handbag, the lipstick, the hairdo, the luggage, and the husband to match.

Today's Chanel woman has a different idea of how things should look. *Elle* magazine reports that Maureen Chiquet, Chanel USA's new president, mixes high and low in a modern way. Her daily uniform is high heels, faded jeans, and a tank top, polished off with a Chanel couture tweed jacket and accessorized with chain-link belts and silver pendants. Chiquet defines the new Chanel woman as rooted in classicism yet "forever modern." She sums up her approach saying, "I've always been a rule breaker" and "I'd love for American women to understand that Chanel was one of the most important risk takers of her time."

No wonder it's cool to wear Old Navy with new Gucci, Hanes T-shirts with Armani suits, fur stoles with cargo pants and turtlenecks—even Converse high-tops with tuxedos. These days, Westchester mansions are filled with flea market finds. We show off our Michael Graves teakettle from Target in our gourmet kitchens, which might even include cabinets purchased from IKEA.

It's no surprise, then, that around this same time, prominent designers such as Todd Oldham and Isaac Mizrahi began courting discounters such as Target to sell their designs. *Time* magazine featured a double truck spread of a Michael Graves toilet brush cleaner in an article on design. Philippe Starck designed elaborately chic hotel rooms for Ian Schrager's budget hotels and personal care products for Japanese 7-Eleven stores. Karl Lagerfeld created a fashion frenzy in the fall of 2004 when he designed a women's sportswear line exclusively for the cheap-chic fashion emporium H&M. About the same time, Costco became a place to treasure hunt for Hugo Boss cashmere sweaters, not just a big box warehouse store where you went to in order to save a few cents on a case of peanut butter. A new genre of retailing came to prominence and the "upscale discounter" was born. Now *there's* a paradox.

CONTRADICTIONS EVERYWHERE

It seemed to me that by the late nineties, everywhere I looked I saw contradictory trends as consumers pursued opposites simultaneously. Just as video-game sales skyrocketed, sales of old-fashioned board games took off too. While Sony racked up sales of PlayStation, Cranium became a huge hit. Hasbro began promoting Family Game Nights on the Internet as sales of long-beloved board games such as Monopoly, Scrabble, and Candy Land surged. Consumers craved blips and bytes as well as cardboard and dice.

Cars got bigger and more in-your-face (Hummers and super-size SUVs) and smaller and cuter (the VW Beetle and the Mini Cooper) at the same time. Modern microwaves and retro-inspired Viking Ranges coexisted peacefully in today's modern kitchens. Fast food restaurants proliferated, and the Slow Food Movement took off. Our waistlines increased, but so did membership in health clubs across the country. Extreme sports such as rock climbing, kite surfing, and snowboarding took off at the same time that simpler hobbies such as bird watching and scrapbooking enjoyed a major revival.

Today, our homes keep getting bigger, even though the average American family is getting smaller. In 1970, the average new single-family house was fourteen hundred square feet; today, it's twenty-three hundred. Today's McMansions feature spa bathrooms, state-of-the-art kitchens, luxury laundry rooms, and gorgeous garages. But at the other end of the size spectrum is the best-selling book *The Not So Big House* by Minnesota architect

Sarah Susanka. Her simple message—that quality should come before quantity—has sparked a movement that is changing the way many Americans think about their homes. Susanka shows homeowners how to downsize their dream house without diminishing the dream. Dream big. Think small. Be happy. Another paradox? In this world of multiplying abundance, bigger is not necessarily better. Less can in fact be more.

On a parallel note, malls around the country are now so big they practically need their own zip codes. The Mall of America in Bloomington, Minnesota, consists of 4.2 million square feet, making it the largest entertainment and retail complex in the country. It houses more than five hundred stores, along with myriad restaurants and entertainment facilities including an aquarium, a twenty-screen movie theater, a theme park, and a wedding chapel. There is even a special parking lot for the RVs that roll into town from North and South Dakota every back-to-school shopping season. They set up camp right in the mall parking lot, hook up to the electrical outlets provided, and they're off to shop.

Although for those consumers, bigger may be better on one given day, those same consumers may prefer a more charming shopping venue on another. Developers are now building lifestyle malls that seek to replicate the Main Street concept from the fifties and sixties, complete with curving cobbled streets and picket fences. It's like shopping just down the street from home.

Travel has its unique paradoxes as well. The wealthy take private helicopters to their favorite bits of wilderness where they sleep under canvas. Fashionistas take a budget airline to Nice and, with the money they "save," spend a weekend at Le Byblos in Saint Tropez. Hilton Hotel ads promise to "take you to the level of care reserved for celebrity, while maintaining your anonymity." We used to resign ourselves to the idea that you can't have it both ways. But in many cases, that's exactly what we're demanding—and *getting.*

Somewhere along the line we became, according to *British Elle*, "the Ecstasy and Echinacea generation." Those who insist on eating only the best organic natural foods today think nothing at all of injecting themselves with Botox (essentially a form of botulism) to help nature along a bit.

THE SCHIZOPHRENIC CONSUMER

Michael Silverstein and Neil Fiske effectively profile this new schizophrenic consumer in their book *Trading Up: The New American Luxury.* They describe a Prada-clad woman driving a Mercedes going to Costco to stock up on her bulk paper goods. While there, she picks up a case of Dom Perignon, at a significant savings. Silverstein and Fiske also introduce us to Joe Six-pack, a construction worker earning $50,000 a year. Joe drinks whatever beer is on sale and dines frequently at McDonald's to save money. But when it comes to golf—his passion—he thinks nothing of spending thousands of dollars on top-of-the-line equipment.

Bottom line, it's become hip to contradict. David Brooks points out in his book *Bobos in Paradise: The New Upper Class and How They Got There* that today's "Bobos," short for "bourgeois bohemians," see nothing contradictory in the fact that they are fanatical about recycling but love driving their gas-guzzling SUVs. Detroit, by the way, recently delivered the perfect product in response to that paradox: the new Ford Escape, a compact hybrid SUV! A paradox on top of an oxymoron.

THE PARADOX OF TOO MUCH CHOICE

So if there isn't one *next big thing,* just what is it that we should all be looking for? I suggest we look at opposite ends of the trend spectrum in order to spot the paradoxes. Charles Handy once said, "The more turbulent the times, the more complex the world, the more paradoxes there are." These days, success belongs to those who learn to embrace complexity by reconciling the contradictions. One need only pick up a newspaper, tune into the nightly news, or attempt to follow the stock market's ups and downs to confirm the turbulent times we live in. With regard to choice, today's consumers have access to an unprecedented number of options, and the task of choosing can be complicated and even overwhelming.

Take the grocery business, for example. If you could time travel back a hundred years or so and enter a typical A&P store somewhere in America, you would discover fewer than three hundred items stocked on its shelves. When I grocery shop today, there are probably three hundred choices on the cereal aisle alone. In fact, the average number of SKUs in the typical grocery store has roughly doubled in the last decade. Today, there are upward of thirty thousand items to choose from. Confusing? Yes. Challenging? You bet!

The choice-challenged might also have a difficult time at Starbucks. The chain that caffeinates the world prides itself on offering customers an endless variety of customizable options. There are eleven kinds of syrup, six kinds of milk, multiple size options (tall, grande, vente), not to mention extra shots, foam–no foam, "wet," extra hot, to go, for here, etc. Regional marketing manager Jerry Thorpe estimates that there may be in the neighborhood of nineteen thousand ways to order a cup of coffee at Starbucks. Perhaps you'd be interested in a nonfat half-caff-triple-grande quarter-sweet sugar-free vanilla nonfat-lactaid extra-hot extra-foamy caramel macchiato—a theoretical worst-drink-order-scenario conjured up by some off-duty Starbucks baristas and posted on the blog paulsop.com.

To help put customers in charge of their choices, Starbucks actually created an eighteen-page booklet that deciphers all the options. It even includes a worksheet that enables customers to present their order to the barista in the correct sequence! Sound complex? Yes, it is, but customers have embraced the lingo, and the proof is in the profits.

Consumers may actually *like* choices—perhaps because they offer new ideas, new possibilities, and new options for expressing their individuality.

Have a notion to buy a new car? Here are some statistics that just might drive you crazy. In 2002, *BusinessWeek* did a special report on car design. In 1995, there were only 909 different cars and light trucks sold in the United States. By 2002, that number rose 44 percent to 1,314.

Carmakers rushed to fill every possible niche in the market, believing that the road to success is paved with endless choice. On top of that, automakers are now offering an endless array of customizable options to those models. Crash ahead? It all depends on how you look at things, but you should definitely fasten your seat belts.

Whether you're buying something as simple as shoes or as complicated as a retirement portfolio, paradoxes abound. Barry Schwartz, in his book *The Paradox of Choice: Less Is More,* points out that faced with too many choices, customers may be so afraid they're not going to make the right choice that they just "decide not to decide."

At the Institute for International Research's Reinventing Consumer Packaged Goods Summit in 2004, J. Walter Smith, president of Yankelovich Partners, highlighted one of the great conundrums of the current retail climate. He said that consumers are beginning to react to a "claustrophobia of abundance." Is it possible that we may actually prefer to have fewer options rather than more?

"THE CHURNING OCEAN OF MILK"

I recently traveled to Siem Riep in Cambodia to visit the ancient temple of Angkor Wat. Built in the twelfth century, Angkor Wat was the world's largest religious building when it was completed, and it remains the world's largest religious complex even today.

"The Churning Ocean of Milk," Angkor Wat, Cambodia

What could this ancient Khmer monument in a beleaguered Southeast Asian country teach me about paradox?

On the eastern gallery of the temple there's a fifty-foot tableau called the "Churning Ocean of Milk." The ancient carving tells the story of eighty-eight gods and ninety-two demons. They are engaged in an endless tug of war, pulling on the body of a giant *naga*—or five-headed snake—suspended over an ocean of milk. It's a battle that continues for all time without fail.

My guide in Angkor Wat explained that this carving represents a story of the "redemption of a stinking world." Back and forth, back and forth, the gods and demons pull on the body of the snake. In the process, they stir up the sea of milk so that the fresh milk constantly rises to the surface. Were the churning to cease, according to the legend, the milk would turn sour.

Put another way, the tug of war embraces opposites and celebrates the necessity of paradox in our lives. It illustrates an attempt to make the world new again by balancing the opposing forces in a way that keeps the world fresh and vital.

Let's explore this lesson in today's business world—let's look at Burberry. Since 1856, Burberry has enjoyed a solidly staid reputation as a maker of high-quality, waterproof raincoats, and counted Her Majesty the Queen among its loyal customers. In the past ten years or so, however, Burberry has churned up the status quo and embraced a new view. Today, their trademark red, camel, white, and black–checked plaid has become a fashion icon—used not only on raincoats, but on every imaginable hat, glove, and other accessory—and even on bikinis.

THE TAO OF TREND

Lao-tzu, ancient Chinese sage, understood the essence of paradox long before Angkor Wat was built. He's credited with writing the *Tao Te Ching,* the book of the ancient way, more than twenty-five hundred years ago. Taoism is one of the three great philosophic teachings of China, based around a concept of duality, or polarity.

Unlike our Western religions and philosophies, where we tend to have contrasting extremes—such as heaven and hell, good and evil, pleasure and pain—Eastern-based philosophies tend not to stress differences. Instead, they stress unity and the interrelationship of all things—especially opposites. This is the concept that the yin and yang symbol represents and embodies.

Lest you begin to think I'm trying to foist off a new (or very, very old) religion on you, let me explain further. Taoism is not an ideology or a new age movement. Rather, it's a living philosophy, a way of thinking and of looking at the world. When all is said and done, Taoism is about being comfortable with change, and change, if you think about it, is the only constant.

Lao-tzu said, "When opposites supplement each other, everything is harmonious." The *Tao Te Ching* teaches us that wisdom is derived from paradox, and paradox is a result of contradictions in our observations and conclusions. To Lao-tzu, contradictions often reveal a deep truth, but to modern science, contradictions indicate an error. Personally, I'm with Lao-tzu on this one.

Embracing this philosophy can help point the way out of a retail environment that is obsessed with touting "the next big thing." It propels us toward a new philosophy where we learn to live with opposites and embrace paradox. In one instance, providing consumers a multitude of options may be appropriate. In another, a single choice may suffice. It is the challenge of each marketer to wrestle with his or her own paradoxes—to ponder what matters most to the specific target audience.

EMBRACING PARADOX

F. Scott Fitzgerald once said that "the test of a first-class mind is the ability to hold two opposing ideas in the head at the same time and still be able to function." It's my belief that at the heart of every consumer, there is a paradox. Psychologists tell us that there are two basic human desires: There is the desire to fit in, to belong to something. It might be a family, a tribe, an organization, a club, a cult, or even a gang. At the opposite end of the spectrum is the second basic human desire: the desire we all have to stand out, to be perceived as an individual, a unique being unlike any other on the planet.

The chapters that follow will take a look at several examples and key macro trends in the marketplace that at first glance appear to be strictly contradictory and not at all harmonious. Upon further investigation, however—if you can hold two opposing ideas in your head at the same time—they provide insights and ideas that, by the very essence of their paradox, can inspire new ideas.

Many companies get caught in the trap of trying to identify the *one right answer* to the question "What will be the next big thing?" when there may not be only one best method or one optimal approach. Perhaps it flies in the face of conventional wisdom in today's business world to abandon our black-and-white thinking and choose, instead, to inhabit the gray area. And yet, by embracing whatever contradictions you may be facing, I am confident the *right* answers will ultimately make themselves known.

I'm always quick to point out that I don't necessarily have the answers to all of your marketing challenges. I do, however, have some worthy insights and some unique ideas that I am confident will help you to see the world with new eyes. You, the experts of your own businesses, will need to look for specific ways to embrace the paradoxes that make up your world, and offer your customers a fresh perspective on your own business.

CHAPTER 2
EVERYTHING OLD IS NEW AGAIN

THE OLD ADAGE "EVERYTHING OLD IS NEW AGAIN" HAS never been more apt. It seems that the more technologically advanced our modern world becomes, the more many of us are interested, intrigued, and enticed by things reminiscent of a slower, simpler, and saner past.

Nostalgia used to be the preserve of the elderly. Today, everyone from kids to teenagers to generations X and Y—in other words, not *just* the baby boomers—are enjoying a trip down memory lane. In this chapter, our own trip includes stops along the way in categories such as food, fashion, transportation and travel, sports and leisure, as well as arts and literature. We'll take a look at how companies and individuals are capitalizing on our newfound fondness for the oldies but goodies.

Marcel Proust once said, "The real voyage of discovery consists of not finding new worlds, but of seeing the world with new eyes." Marketers today are doing far more than just finding and resurrecting "old stuff." The current voyage of discovery involves translating an idea or brand or product from the past in a new way that makes sense for today's world.

TRANSPORTATION AND TRAVEL:
On the Road Again

Given all the state-of-the-art engineering advancements, high-tech safety features, burgeoning hybrid technology, and break-throughs in computerized designing capabilities, we should all be driving utilitarian, podlike vehicles devoid of any unnecessary adornments. But instead, consumers are finding resonance with designs that hearken back to a saner, simpler time.

MINI COOPER

The Mini Cooper is a real star on the road and on the big screen as well, having been featured in the 2004 hit movie *The Italian Job*. More than forty thousand Minis were sold in the United States in 2004 alone—which represents a roughly 20 percent increase from the previous year's sales. While the Mini waiting list grows longer each day, the Mini is really just the latest in a long line of vehicles that have capitalized on the "old is new" concept.

The trend started with the restyled VW Beetle and gained momentum with Chrysler's roadster-inspired PT Cruiser. Wolfsburg (Germany) and Detroit were among the first to understand the value of looking back when designing the future. However,

Volkswagen and Chrysler didn't merely copy designs of the past, these manufacturers tailored their cars to today's modern lifestyle. In addition to technological improvements, they added touches aimed at pushing what I refer to as magic buttons—features that surprise and delight customers and allow them to express their individuality. For example, Volkswagen stuck a bud vase on the dashboard of their Beetle, and the PT Cruiser offers a roomy interior and a funky assortment of colors. But they're not the only companies that breathed new life into some old designs.

VESPA

Originally designed to give Italians a cheap way to get around a war-torn country, the Vespa scooter has made a fashionable comeback—this time in the American market.

In post–WWII Italy, both the economy and the roads were in sad shape. People needed an easy, inexpensive mode of transportation. Piaggio delivered a fashionable and practical solution. Glamorous from the start, the Vespa got a boost when Gregory Peck took Audrey Hepburn for a spin around Rome in the 1953 movie *Roman Holiday*. The sleek steel body and sexy curves, not to mention the cute candy colors, made it an instant hit for the fashion crowd. The scooter was simple and well designed. The enclosed engine, bench seat, bicycle handlebars, and protected footboards combined to give the Vespa a cleaner, more comfortable ride than a motorcycle.

Four years ago, the Vespa (the Italian word for "wasp") made a triumphant return to American shores, after being banned in the eighties for not meeting U.S. emissions standards. The new, environmentally improved scooter is now sold in "boutiques" (not dealerships) around the country. The newly hip Vespa brand rose to prominence in the mass domain when Matthew Broderick was featured in *People* magazine on the new model, a birthday present from his wife, Sarah Jessica Parker. Gwyneth Paltrow has one, and so does Robert DeNiro.

LA DOLCE VITA

The Italian design influence is also big news Down Under. Last year, retro glamour arrived in Sydney Harbor in the form of La Dolce Vita, a classic Italian wooden boat reminiscent in elegance and glamour of the movie star era of the 1950s and 1960s. Think Cary Grant and Grace Kelly speeding along the French Riviera in *To Catch a Thief.*

La Dolce Vita—Italian for "the sweet life"—is at the heart of much of the nostalgic resurgence now taking place. However, while we long for quieter, simpler times, we still demand a cushy, refined reinterpretation of the good old days. In Sydney, the La Dolce Vita luxury water limousine may reflect the glamour of a bygone age, but the new boats are very much a product of the twenty-first century. Fast, powerful, sleek, and beautiful, the boats are hand built, made of mahogany, and fitted with a powerful engine and every modern convenience.

FASHION: The Way We Were . . . Only Better

The world of fashion continuously mines decades past for inspiration for the collections of the future, but this method works best when the fashion isn't a literal copy of that bygone era. The most successful designers manage to translate the ideas into a look or item in a signature way that relates to today's modern lifestyles. For the autumn winter 2006–2007 designer collections, designers ranging from Gucci to Ghost," Carolina Herrera to Max Mara, all took a trip back in time to the seventies and resurrected the maxi coat. It happens every season.

Brands like Ocean Pacific evoke vintage sixties surf culture and Wrangler Jeans mine the old West. Is there ever really any true *newness* in fashion? Or isn't it mostly a modern-day reinterpretation of older styles?

RALPH LAUREN

Perhaps no designer capitalizes on the "old is new" approach better than Ralph Lauren does. Personally, when I want a new golf outfit, business suit, or comfy flannel pajamas, I can count on Ralph Lauren's adeptness at reinterpreting classic designs in fresh, modern ways.

Ralph Lauren is a master of memory marketing. His multiple brands transport you back to a time when clothes made the man—or woman—and *class* was the order of the day. So even if you aren't an Ivy Leaguer, a wealthy philanthropist, or living in a huge mansion, you can dress as though you are.

In the summer of 2005, Ralph Lauren Blue Label featured the New Oxford Shirt in glossy fashion magazines such as *Elle* and *Vogue*. The ads featured a beautiful, aristrocratic, athletic-looking woman wearing a grass-green oxford shirt with the Polo pony logo knotted pirate style at her slim waist. The rest of her outfit consisted of a tiny floral-print bikini. Her long hair was windblown from a day at the beach; she was living the good life, no doubt.

The copy read, "The new, skinny fit, Blue Label oxford shirt, in sexy summer colors." Period. When you get down to the technicalities, an oxford shirt is an oxford shirt, and it's been around a long time. But it really did look new again, thanks to great styling and clever marketing.

Just recently, Ralph Lauren announced another line designed to evoke an era when preppy looks ruled the schools. Ralph Lauren Rugby was developed from scratch with a vertically integrated retail concept to appeal to the fashion-forward college student whose childhood is rooted in preppy looks. It's *not* meant to resurrect a preppy fashion statement.

The new fashion collection targets the eighteen- to twenty-five-year-old college and postcollege graduate, and includes rugby shirts, polos, sweaters, denim jeans and khakis, jackets, suits, outerwear, and accessories, all at 40 percent below Blue Label retails. The first store opened in Boston on Newbury Street in October 2004. Additional stores are located in Charlottesville, Virginia; Chapel Hill, North Carolina; New York City; New Canaan, Connecticut; and Georgetown, Washington, D.C.

The twenty-five-hundred-square-foot stores evoke a collegiate setting from another era, with hardwood floors, a rugby scoreboard, and billiard tables. In other words, it's about as far away from a high-tech, sleek, modern environment as you can possibly get.

NIKE

Nike is known for cutting-edge technology and for injecting high-tech functionality into footwear fashions. These days, they are making a splash on college campuses—and *not* just in the locker rooms. They've scored big time in making the old new again.

They recently resurrected three sneaker models from their archives: the Pocketknife, the Blazer, and the Vandal Supreme. These shoes evoke the early high-top basketball looks of the 1950s. They are well-trod styles that now replace the standard leather or canvas (think Converse style) uppers with hand-woven classic Harris Tweed fabrics.

Harris Tweed is usually associated with a stroll on the Scottish moors, grouse-hunting parties, or your grandfather's old wear-everywhere sport coat (the one with the woven leather buttons and suede elbow patches). It's not something that the big men on campus usually associate with "cool."

Nike's request for ten thousand yards of the official fabric was the largest single order in the history of the Scottish Harris Tweed Authority. For centuries, the inhabitants of the Scottish

Outer Hebrides islands have made the cloth entirely by hand. How interesting that today, this fabric that represents a tradition from time immemorial is making fashion headlines on college campuses around our country.

OLYMPIC RETRO

Shoes are a particularly personal part of one's wardrobe. They clearly indicate something about who we are, where we come from, and what we think. We express ourselves through our footwear, and Nike isn't the only manufacturer figuring out which magic buttons to push.

One current nostalgia craze involves the Olympics. It seems the 2004 Summer Olympic Games sparked a renewed interest in all things Olympic. Because the games were held in Greece, the birthplace of the ancient games as well as the venue for the first Olympics held in the modern era (1896), the nostalgia pull was especially strong. Worth Global Style Network (WGSN) reported on several athletic shoe brands that capitalized on this "everything old is new again" trend.

Reebok offered a limited-edition launch of the J. W. Foster shoe based on a running spike from 1895 (think *Chariots of Fire*). The retro-style shoe was rendered in authentic brown leather and the original branding and featured an old-fashioned soccer-style tongue.

The United Kingdom–based Oki-Ni continued its collaboration with Adidas and relaunched the 1968 classic Antelope Trainer in directional metallic shades of gold, silver, and bronze, in strictly limited numbers. The high-priced shoes were a run-away hit on the Internet.

Lastly, Zeha—one of the oldest trainer brands in the world, which for all practical purposes disappeared when the Berlin Wall went up—was revived in 2004 by two enterprising Berliners. They faithfully reproduced many of the original designs featuring the brand's striking double-stripe emblem and subsequently became one of Germany's post-unification business successes.

As WGSN style editors commented, "Part of the passion of the sports world is our enthusiasm for the modern and the new, blended with many memories and nostalgic associations with previous sporting occasions." They went on to point out that the Olympic Games more than likely provide designers with "a lifetime's inspiration."

VINTAGE T-SHIRTS

A friend of mine was at a concert recently and told me about the vintage T-shirts various club kids were wearing. One girl who was wearing a Clash T-shirt was definitely too young to have been around when The Clash was rocking the casbah more than two decades ago. Chances are, her parents introduced her to a band they'd enjoyed since they were her age. Personally, I didn't enjoy the music my parents allegedly listened to when they were young—and you *never* would have caught me wearing, say, a Dinah Shore T-shirt to a concert.

It's fascinating that today's tech-savvy kids are harkening

back to a time they can't even remember. But just go on eBay and you will discover vintage T-shirts from cult seventies' television shows such as *Charlie's Angels, Dukes of Hazzard,* and *ChiPs* selling for a premium. And, on the heels of a successful low-budget film called *Harold and Kumar Go to White Castle,* sales of White Castle T-shirts with logos and slogans such as Always Open, Always Tasty were instant best sellers at stores ranging from Dillard's to the Buckle.

HOME: Not-So-Modern Living

We live in a world where modern architecture is greatly prized and acknowledged, not to mention rewarded. Many of the best contemporary architects, such as Frank Gehry and Santiago Calatrava, have been dubbed "starchitects" and have been raised to cultlike celebrity status, as have their thoroughly futuristic, cutting-edge designs.

Back in the fifties, when futurists were asked to describe what the home of the next century would look like, they more often than not described a Jetsons-like environment—sleek, robotic, and ultraefficient. But, in fact, the majority of today's homes are anything but. In my home, I have state-of-the-art wireless entertainment hookups and all the latest appliances and gadgetry, and yet my kitchen resembles my grandmother's, my living room expresses a British colonial *Out of Africa* sensibility, and the centerpiece of my great room is a wood-burning fireplace that I absolutely cherish. It seems that although many of us live in the city, our homes often belong to the country and to another era. The Audit Bureau of Circulations confirms that two of the biggest shelter magazines in the country are *Country Home* and *Country Living*.

The *New York Times* recently featured a story titled "Crumbled to Perfection." In it, the author observed, "Prada-clad fashionistas may shudder, but country style is back on the radar." The article went on to profile several modern families that chose to embrace this crumbled to perfection paradox. "Some people are content to visit ruins," he said. "Some prefer to live in them full time."

Hard to picture? Just think of the treasures awaiting you at Anthropologie, the chic upscale cousin of Urban Outfitters. Anthropologies's mission is to raid the flea markets and attics of the world to come up with new things purposefully designed to look old. And note that I didn't say old-fashioned.

Same idea with Shabby Chic, the Rachel Ashwell home fashion emporium that has helped make washed linen, slipcovers, antique chandeliers, and overstuffed chairs and sofas all the rage, everywhere from minimalist lofts to country homes and beach cottages.

Decorators say part of the appeal of the crumbled to perfection sensibility is that it makes our living environment eminently comfortable. It evokes a time when things were more real and less rushed. That's why vintage is so trendy right now. It's all about feeling "at home."

SARAH CIHAT: REHABILITATED CHINA

Sarah Cihat, a Brooklyn-based graduate of New York's Parson's School of Design, is serving up second helpings—of old china, that is. She describes her line, Fifty-Cents, as "rehabilitated dishware." Sarah buys up old and mismatched china at Salvation Army thrift stores and from estate sales and artfully revives them with mosaiclike patterns in fresh-colored glazes. She credits "grandmothers and bad art" as her inspiration. Think skull-adorned creamers and rock-star serving platters, all freshly rendered in funky colors ranging from apricot to aqua to candy pink.

Sarah's approach may be radical as well as tongue-in-cheek, but part of her motivation is ecologically inspired. She's passionate about *not* just filling up the world with more "stuff." From trash to treasures, one person's "That old stuff" is another's "Wow, check this out!"

TUPPERWARE

Venture out of the city and into a more suburban zip code and you will find a soccer mom who moonlights as a Tupperware representative. It might surprise you to learn that every 2.5 seconds, somewhere in the world a special party begins with a burp. The burp, of course, is the familiar noise made when the venerable Tupperware bowl or container is sealed.

I remember dreading the sole Tupperware party I attended back in the early eighties. Because a dear friend of mine was hosting it, I overcame my trepidation and showed up on time and even bought a set of Popsicle molds (a brilliant selection, considering I don't have kids). Those unused Tupperware molds became a garage sale bargain many years later.

Today, 50 million people a year attend Tupperware parties around the globe, and annual sales have topped the $1 billion mark. Today's parties are no longer limited to suburbia, however. Turns out the hip Manhattan-urbanite crowd loves their Tupperware, too. Thanks to sexy fresh designs, a new generation of working moms, and a later time slot (many parties now take place at the cocktail hour, when cosmopolitans are served instead of tea). I can actually see myself *wanting* to be invited to one of these gatherings.

GHOST OF LOUIS

If you were to venture into a chic flat in Paris or a fashionable apartment in Milan, you might expect to see classic furniture designed in the elegant and prestigious style of Louis XVI. But chances are, you wouldn't expect to see it rendered in transparent injection-molded polycarbonate. Surprise! Philippe Starck's "Ghost of Louis" chair for Kartel is a stacking chair available in an array of colors ranging from gray smoke to straw yellow to crystal clear. The chair is reported to be one of the best-selling seating SKUs in the Design Within Reach catalog.

It's clear that Starck is a master at reinventing the classic. His playful version of a Louis XVI armchair is described in that same Design Within Reach catalog as "a robust chair with not a single weak point that will blend into any background while retaining their hint of wit and elegance." No wonder the design magazines call it "the little black dress of seating." And we all know how many versions of that wardrobe staple are still being designed and sold as "the perfect dress for any occasion."

LITERATURE: The Greatest Story Ever Resold

When Oprah Winfrey announced that she was discontinuing her book club, I was as disappointed as her other fans were—to say nothing of the book publishers who had profited greatly when Oprah selected one of their current titles. Everyone celebrated Oprah's decision to revive the book club, which initially incorporated an "old is new" twist. Her first selection, John Steinbeck's 1952 classic, *East of Eden,* rode the best-seller lists that first summer. The following year, *Anna Karenina* was selected, and even the girls on *Sex in the City* were reading it at the beach.

The spillover effect was swift and strong. Publishing houses such as Penguin and retailers such as the giant Barnes & Noble began to repackage and revitalize their stable of classics. *Jane Eyre, Don Quixote, Siddhartha,* as well as works by Proust, Dumas, Stendhal, and Balzac, were all dusted off for a new generation. Same story, new twist.

There's a happy ending to this story for book-sellers and publishing houses as well. You see, this genre of books is often out of copyright, so profit margins are often as fat as the books are thick.

NANCY DREW

When I was a child growing up, the only good thing about getting sick, besides staying home from school, was that it usually meant a new Nancy Drew mystery to read. Back then, Nancy searched for clues in the old oak tree out in the backyard, but she's come a long way since I was a kid. Today, Nancy is still around, but now she drives a hybrid car. She and her boyfriend, Ned, take flying lessons. She searches for clues on the Internet and sports a hip wardrobe that JLo would love. Girls in tune with Lindsay Lohan are now discovering the appeal of the smart, fashionable, and clever girl sleuth. There's even a Web-based fan club, www.nancydrewsleuth.com, and a movie in the works. It's not your grandmother's Nancy, that's for sure.

DICK AND JANE

"See Dick run. Run, Dick, run." Those six words conjure up larger-than-life memories for the baby-boomer crowd. Most of us (yes, I'll admit I'm one) fondly remember learning to read in the 1950s from the classic grade-school primer.

Well, no surprise here. The brother and sister duo, along with their baby sister, Sally, and America's favorite spaniel, Spot, are back. *Growing Up with Dick and Jane* is a new sampler of stories and cut outs repackaged by Pearson that traces the history of the Dick and Jane phenomenon from their birth during the Depression to their retirement in the sixties.

The newly released anthology takes you back "to a time where night never comes, knees never scrape, parents never yell, and fun never stops." The entertaining and informative text tracks important historical, social, and educational events of the Dick and Jane era. Who could resist the opportunity to relive the memories of home, school, and what it was like to grow up when childhood felt like one long summer day?

THE ART OF WRITING

Futurists once predicted that we would become a paperless society thanks to the advent of e-mail and the Internet. Chicken Littles everywhere bemoaned the end of books, along with handwritten correspondence, fine pens, and elegant handmade stationery. A recent article in Hyatt's *Destination* magazine reassures us that that's just not going to happen. It notes that "whether personally or professionally, the very act of taking the time to pen a note by hand speaks volumes and stands out."

Clearly, e-mail has brought us real-time convenience, but it has also brought the added hassles of unwanted spam and pesky computer viruses. How ironic, then, that the logical "replacement" for pen and paper in reality served to reinforce our love of—and need for—a tactile experience with the real thing. Here we are in the "age of the Internet," and fine stationers and luxury paper goods companies are having a heyday selling bespoke note cards and archival-quality 100 percent cotton papers. These papers are personalized by hand-engraving them with steel rather than copper, or copying them on a computer.

Mont Blanc is also capitalizing on this trend/countertrend phenomenon. Their recent ads show the classic fountain pen proudly standing at attention in a stand, proclaiming "New since 1927," which nails the paradox on the head. (The white star logo represents the snowcapped mountain as in *Mont Blanc*: "white mountain.")

SPORTS AND LEISURE: Recess Redux

As high-tech toys and electronic gadgets proliferate, it's ironic that in gymnasiums and playgrounds as well as at corporate team-building events around the country, old-fashioned childhood games are being revived at a breakneck speed. It is also ironic that in this workaholic age where parents are busy shuttling kids to piano lessons and soccer matches that there is a growing focus on how to spend our ever-briefer leisure time.

DODGEBALL

I'm not a sports enthusiast, in general, but a recent *USA Today* cover story caused me to have a flashback to my fifth-grade gym class. "Just saying dodgeball takes you back to your childhood," the article declared. For me, it takes me back to the school playground, where I desperately hoped I would not be the last person picked for the dodgeball team. It was clearly less about exercise and more about fitting in. Today, however, dodgeball is not only a favored recreational activity for young people, it has also become an often-used team-building exercise in the business world.

Turns out all that dodging, ducking, and running provides a

real aerobic workout. *Elle* magazine did a short piece on how gyms nationwide are encouraging us to "regress to grade school behavior" by offering workouts inspired by recess activities from our childhood. Dodgeball cardio classes have proliferated, as have official dodgeball societies. *Fortune* magazine reported on how trendsetting sports aficionados (Ben Affleck for one) have resurrected the game of dodgeball. Of course, the game looks a lot different from what it did when I was a kid. While we wore gym shorts, baggy T-shirts, and Converse sneakers, today's players wear kneepads and protective Lycra clothing with distinctive logos and graphics similar to motocross attire.

Nowadays, teams of twenty try to blast opponents with as many as eight big red rubber balls, each one flying at once, and coed matches take place to a hip-hop soundtrack. Popular media may have started the dodgeball resurrection. The reality dating series *Average Joe* staged a game between the "hunks" and the "geeks" (the hunks won). In the summer of 2004, Twentieth Century Fox released the comedy *Dodgeball*, starring Ben Stiller and Vince Vaughn. It wasn't exactly a "hit," but that hasn't stopped many Americans from going back to the gym or the playground for a little nostalgic exercise.

DOUBLE DUTCH

WGSN did a trend report on double Dutch skip roping, "a sport intrinsically linked with hip-hop and New York street culture" that's currently enjoying a revival in pop videos, films, and style magazines.

Originally it was an inexpensive game played by schoolchildren, popular at the same time as hopscotch and capture the flag. Very little equipment was needed, and it could be played anywhere there was a concrete or tar surface. In the 1970s, it became popular as a sport, and in the 1980s, it received worldwide notice when music innovator Malcolm McLaren released a track titled "Double Dutch."

Today's version is complex and showy, with moves interpreted from break dancing, acrobatics, and skateboarding incorporated into theatrically choreographed freestyle routines. Teams compete against one another for prizes and trophies in special competitions. The specialized moves have names such as lifted aerial, suicide in, helicopter, caterpillar, disco swing, brain washer, and awesome Annie.

It's not only glamorous, it's physically demanding. Wouldn't it be great if double Dutch jumping could jump-start a countertrend to the obesity epidemic that is jeopardizing our kids' health and well-being today?

BASKETBALL

While dodgeball and double Dutch are examples of actual games being reinvented, there are instances where a redesign of a game's accoutrements can lead to revitalized sales and a boost for the sport itself. One would think that there wasn't much opportunity to redesign a basketball. It must be round and it has to bounce, but Nike added luster to the game when they came up with the Go Pro Shooting System.

I.D. magazine awarded the new basketball with a design award in 2005. The Go Pro ball "features recessed rubber 'shot dots' that serve as fingertip guides and a pattern of oblong yellow shapes that spin into a solid line when the ball is properly launched." The Nike designers took a tactile and visual approach in order to help young players acquire an effective grip and release giving an old ball a new bounce.

TOYS AND GAMES: Games People (Still) Play

Even our play incorporates aspects of "everything old is new again." The world of tech toys is hotter than ever, but so is that of redesigned retro favorites. In recent holiday seasons, kids clamored for classics such as Strawberry Shortcake, My Little Pony, and Care Bears. The citizens of Weebleville returned with a bright new look, and there were even occasional shortages of Cabbage Patch dolls. Most of these classics returned with new bells and whistles and electronic gadgetry attached, or offered some special customizable option.

The Retro Rocket is both beautiful and fun, and while it may not take you to the moon, it will deliver you to another warm and fuzzy time. Radio Flyer brought back the old-fashioned ride-on toy, and it competes successfully with the new pint-size Hummer electronic "vehicle" that indulgent grandparents buy for their grandkids.

Technology may have its thrills, but board games offer their own unique rewards. While most video games are played solo, part of the appeal of board games is that they bring people together. According to the NPD group, a global market research leader in sales data and marketing information, in 2003 board games sales were $1.04 billion, up from the previous year. Monopoly is still one of the most popular board games in the world, offered in twenty-six languages and sold in more than eighty countries. Its capitalistic effect is so strong that it's still banned in the Communist states of North Korea and Cuba!

HOMBY TRAINS

Interestingly, it's not just American favorites that are on the comeback track. Sense Worldwide, an online trend bulletin from the United Kingdom notes, "British adults are rushing to buy model train sets on a wave of nostalgia that is helping to power sales of one of Britain's oldest toy companies." The model train company Homby attributes their recent runaway success to the renewed popularity among forty- to fifty-year-olds "who are buying them as a serious hobby." Part of the attraction is the nostalgia factor, but analysts also attribute the interest to the success of Harry Potter and the Hogwarts Express train set. Either way, they're on the right track.

OKO TRICYCLE

Sometimes it takes a whole new design approach, not just a few tweaks, to reinstate and reinvigorate an old classic. Growing up, pretty much every little kid in America had a tricycle. It was a childhood right of passage from the red trike to the new two-wheeler bike, even if it required a few training wheels along the way.

Thanks to OKO, kids today have a brand-new ergonomically designed version of the old classic to get their transportation training permits with. The OKO Tricycle features nine positions for seat and handlebars, a futuristic-looking, cradle-shaped frame that eliminates the need for a crossbar. Easy-to-reach pedals and a molded safety-harnessed neoprene-padded seat make it safe and easy to learn to ride. It even comes with a windowed sunshade and a push handle in the back for Dad to guide with. The $149.95 toy would make even Elroy Jetson feel like a lucky boy.

POKER

Poker's been around a long time. The game was introduced in this country by the riverboats on the Mississippi and Ohio rivers in the 1800s. Who would have ever bet that it would make a comeback such that tournaments are televised, TV shows such as *Celebrity Poker* top the ratings, and sets of playing cards and casino-quality poker chips have become best-selling Christmas gifts? If you'd taken that bet, you'd be a winner. Today, everyone from high school students to Hollywood celebrities is gambling on a good time with every deal of a deck of cards. No wonder books such as *Bad Beats and Lucky Draws: Poker Strategies, Winning Hands, and Stories from the Professional Poker Tour* by Phil Hellmuth, Jr., are topping best-seller lists at bookstores across the country.

VIEW-MASTER RETURNS

The original View-Master, created in 1939 as a way to bring the world to you, could be considered completely outdated in today's digital world of pixels and megabytes. But that's not the case. Last year, Fisher-Price reintroduced a special collector's edition to commemorate the sixty-fifth anniversary of the once-popular toy. The handset looks just as the original did and comes complete with eight reels of footage from the decades since its invention. View-Master can give you a unique perspective on the past, as well as of the future.

FOOD: Just Like Grandma Used to Buy

Comfort food *comforts*. Nothing beats mashed potatoes and gravy, homemade rice pudding, or macaroni and cheese for giving you that much-needed warmth deep down inside. Did you know that Martha Stewart's number one requested recipe from her Web site is for her version of macaroni and cheese?

Scientists may be hard at work on genetically modified foods, additives, and preservatives that make things more nutritious and shelf stable, and "nutraceuticals" and "cosmeceuticals" that promise to make us more beautiful from the inside out. But in reality, most of us are comfortably satisfied with new versions of our old food favorites.

DYLAN'S CANDY BAR

Ralph Lauren's daughter, Dylan, opened Dylan's Candy Bar on Manhattan's very fashionable East Side. It's a thoroughly modern candy store that cleverly reinterprets the old-fashioned candy emporium. For kids, it's a fairy tale fantasy world come true. For adults, it's a trip down memory lane. You can find anything and everything you need to induce a sugar coma here—from giant Pez to Hershey's kisses to Charleston Chews, taffy, and Bit-O-Honey. It's memory marketing at its best. The candy may be an old favorite, but the packaging and presentation are innovative and irresistible.

SPAM

The all-purpose lunch meat made by Hormel Foods has been the butt of jokes and a staple of dorm parties for years, but the 67-year-old brand is now getting a rehash. Product sales in 2004 jumped 10 percent in Britain after a marketing campaign urged Brits to eat their SPAM.

On March 17, 2005, a musical entitled *Spamalot* opened on Broadway. Adapted from the 1975 movie classic *Monty Python and the Holy Grail,* early reviews pegged it as the most eagerly awaited new musical since *The Producers.*

When tickets went on sale on December 6, 2004, the first one hundred delighted fans waiting in line outside New York's Shubert Theatre received a promotional gift of a limited-edition can of Golden Honey Grail SPAM. After its lengthy and relatively nonglamorous existence, SPAM is suddenly enjoying its moment in the spotlight!

RETRO SODAS AND COCKTAILS

In the seventies, Coke famously taught the world to sing, but today, consumers are humming a different tune. While this may *still* be a Coke and Pepsi universe we live in, a variety of regional and retro soda makers have established comfortable and profitable niches in the U.S. beverage market. For example, Cheerwine, a company founded in 1917 in North Carolina, produces a unique cherry cola–flavored soda known by the Cheerwine name. Today, its overall growth is up 20 percent on average, and has been for the last several years. They capitalized on their unique flavor and retro-brand packaging promotions by reintroducing their classic custom-molded glass bottle design from 1957.

Two other retro sodas are also on an expansion roll out: Big Red, a soda from deep in the heart of Texas, with a taste reminiscent of cream soda and bubblegum; and Green River, an eighty-five-year-old lime-tasting concoction available mostly in the Midwest. Their combined success speaks not only to a thirst for nostalgia among aging baby boomers, but to clever marketing and business decisions made by the third- and fourth-generation family owners of the companies.

These companies spend more on their ingredients than the Big Beverage Three, often using real sugar instead of the ubiquitous high fructose corn syrup. Ironically, they can afford to do this because their margins are so high. Because they've been operating for so long, their costly bottling and distribution systems were paid in full decades ago.

The same trend/countertrend developments are evident in the liquor industry, as well. Thanks to the birth of the cosmopolitan martini in the late eighties—and to the drink's endless cameos on *Sex and the City,* there's now an insatiable demand for Day-Glo spin-offs of the classic cocktail.

What's more, martini glasses are the new accessory for the bar. The retro martini glass is an icon, with a link to every pop culture pinup from Frank Sinatra to Dorothy Parker to 007. The martini craze has spawned a huge demand for other retro cocktails, including manhattans, gimlets, sidecars, and pink ladies.

HOME MILK DELIVERY

Got milk? These days it's easier than ever to answer yes! Back in "the good old days," home delivery accounted for most milk sales in the United States. By 1963, it was only about a third. By 2001, it represented a paltry 0.4 percent. But all that's changing. Today, there are dairies all around the country that are struggling to keep pace with demand for home-delivered bottled milk. They are bucking the supercenter trend as they grapple with an unexpected demand that industry officials attribute to nostalgia, convenience, and taste.

Says Mike Forbes, who owns a delivery service, "Once I had maybe four hundred customers in one city. Now I've got eight hundred in two counties." Turns out middle- to upper-class customers are happy to pay a premium for milk from local farms, much of which is produced organically or without the use of added hormones.

FRIED TWINKIES

Twinkies were the surprise in my lunch box back when I still carried my lunch. During summer 2004, they were the surprise of my visit to the Minnesota State Fair. The concept of re-naming mundane old products has now reached the height of novelty with the introduction of the Fried Twinkie.

Hostess Twinkies, sponge cakes filled with frosting, have been a favorite dessert snack of American kids for decades. Some clever entrepreneur came up with idea of coating these treats with batter, freezing them on a stick, deep-frying them, and then dusting them warm from the fryer with powdered sugar.

Unofficial surveys indicate that it may well be the most popular food on a stick at state fairs across the United States, despite the low-carb craze. Who knows, this new twist on an old favorite might even be enough to help Hostess pull itself out of bankruptcy.

TRAVEL: Old Meets New

Many of my favorite places seem to be full of paradoxes. Walk through the ancient stone streets of Florence, Italy, and everyone is carrying a cell phone. Enter Renaissance courtyards, and you will discover apartments filled with modern furniture and Alessi accessories. Wander the colonial streets of San Miguel de Allende in Mexico, and you may well stumble upon an Internet café. In Bilbao, Spain—a once-decaying town on the banks of the Nervión River—the thoroughly modern new Guggenheim museum provides a much-welcomed addition that is fostering new growth. It's always been hip to discover the latest untouched-by-modern-man travel destination, but now these diamonds in the rough are reinventing themselves to attract savvy travelers—without losing their local character.

DUBAI

A few years ago I had the opportunity to speak at an MIT Pan-Arab conference in Dubai, United Arab Emirates. I was stunned and amazed at the paradox the country represented.

Dubai is a modern high-rise city that's become the financial and trading capital of the Arab world, as well as being America and Europe's burgeoning new sports and leisure playland. Tiger Woods plays golf there, Venus and Serena Williams play tennis there, and world-class racers compete in Formula One events in Dubai. It's also a shopper's paradise. I think it's a telling sign that Saks Fifth Avenue recently selected Dubai over London, Paris, and Berlin to open its first international operation there.

In contrast, however, parts of the city still remain firmly entrenched in biblical times. You need only catch a water taxi or hop aboard a sailing *dhow* to cross Dubai Creek (the Khor Dubai), and you are in another place in time. Walk through an early *souk*, where merchants sell embroidered silk fabrics and exotic spices such as frankincense and myrrh. Walk farther through the narrow winding streets and you might eventually come across a camel caravan getting ready to cross into the desert, headed straight for the next oasis.

THE 10TH ARRONDISSEMENT

Just as the "Churning Ocean of Milk" in Angkor Wat, Cambodia, Paris is in an ongoing state of flux. But the area along the quais of Canal Saint-Martin—the 10th Arrondissement—is currently enjoying its moment in the sun. You may remember the actress Audrey Tautou dreamily skipping stones into the canal in the 2001 French hit film *Amélie*.

For decades, travelers to Paris dutifully signed up for a walking tour of Hemingway's Paris, but these days, they hop on the Metro to the 10th arrondissement for a first-person view of Amélie's Paris. They seek a Paris that is more imaginary than real—a nostalgic fairy tale vision of the old-fashioned, yet funky Paris they fell in love with while watching a movie. The *real* place they actually find is both energetic and eclectic—a neighborhood populated by artists, designers, and stylists, where chic new restaurants open next to quaint barbershops, and, according to *Wallpaper* magazine, where the multicultural mix of different ethnic cultures makes the area "more Punjabi than Parisian."

SHADY DELL

If you ever dream of a cross-country road trip in an Airstream, there's a special place waiting for you at the end of the ride. The Shady Dell RV Park, in Bisbee, Arizona, is a rub-your-eyes, am-I-really-here kind of place. On Highway 80, the road that stretches through southern Arizona to San Diego, you'll eventually come to the Shady Dell camping site, established in 1927.

Today, its enterprising owners have made it a thoroughly new experience for the generation that missed the chance to travel the country in a riveted "canned ham" or a silver "bread loaf" (as certain models of the old travel trailers were called). Here, the classic RVs are for rent. They represent more than the sum total of all their various parts—from antique dinnerware, old-style toasters, flowery chenille bedspreads, ten-stool diners, and glaring neon road signs.

The Shady Dell RV Park looks like a scene from a movie, one that you can move right into and sample a bygone era of pure Americana and the fantasy of the open road.

ART: Remakes and Fresh Takes

When addressing an audience at the Walker Art Center in Minneapolis, film director Ang Lee stated that "all art is provocation." He suggested that people are typically in search of quick and easy answers, but that his job as a filmmaker is simply to ask the questions. I agree with Ang Lee. Art *is* a provocation—it can be either about seeing new things or seeing things in a new way.

MATTHEW BOURNE'S *SWAN LAKE*

It's seldom advisable to tamper with a well-loved classic. Imagine you are in a theater and the music from Tchaikovsky's *Swan Lake* begins. You await the arrival of the swans, but instead of the corps de ballet in tutus and toe shoes, out dance a flock of men in wild, feathery chaps.

Directed and choreographed by Matthew Bourne, an avant-garde version of the traditional *Swan Lake* ballet is dancing new life into a traditional story. (You might remember seeing a brief moment from Bourne's production during the final scene in the movie *Billy Elliot,* when the Irish son of a hardscrabble coal miner leaps out onto a stage in whitened face, feathered chaps, and bare chest and feet, and stuns the audience with his grace and power.) In fact, Bourne's *Swan Lake* is the longest running ballet ever in London's West End. It goes to show that you can make the old (even the most well-respected classic) into something new and desirable, if you just rethink the story from a different point of view.

JAY NUHRING'S RESEE GALLERY

Artist Jay Nuhring is owner of the reSee Gallery in Minneapolis. His own work smoothly combines the aesthetic values of design with environmental preservation and what he calls "cultural re-appropriation." It offers the viewer a new way of seeing and ap-preciating an often-overlooked element of the American landscape: the billboard. Jay deconstructs these "found objects," turning fragments of billboard art into new, invigorating, modern works of art. In his hands, an otherwise empty and short-lived medium is rejuvenated and redefined. The reSee Gallery seeks to reinterpret and revitalize popular culture by refocusing perspectives, reframing original material, and reenvisioning the result.

I often take clients on a stroll through Jay Nuhring's reSee Gallery. As a way to challenge their old way of thinking and shake loose some fresh inspiration, I simply ask them to read what's on

Jay Nuhring, owner of reSee Gallery, Minneapolis

the gallery's front window: "reAppropriate, reExperience, re-Interpret, reCycle, reVisit, reView, reNew, reDo."

CONCLUSION

Just as the "Churning Ocean of Milk" does, our modern culture is constantly churning up new ideas in an effort to prevent stagnation—to keep the milk from going sour—and to hold the interest of an easily distracted consumer base. Through the many examples in this chapter, I hope the paradox is clear: Many of our best new ideas are really just old ideas reinterpreted. One could argue that cultural reappropriation has become the standard of our era, and evidence of that is everywhere. Turn on the radio and you will almost certainly hear a familiar seventies' musical riff implanted into a new pop, r&b, or hip-hop hit. Visit the neighborhood cinema mega-plex and what's "Now Showing" is likely a remake, sequel, or pre-quel. (In the case of certain seventies' television shows that were remade into mediocre summer movies, it could also be argued that some of our worst new ideas are really just old ideas, too.)

Perhaps in the face of mass globalization and its attendant concerns, we increasingly find comfort in the familiar, but nostalgia for nostalgia's sake will not suffice. It isn't enough simply to replicate a former success, right down to the last detail. The most successful reincarnations are ones that engage us emotionally and respond directly to our new concerns. In other words, they foster desire in the present.

CHAPTER 3
MASS CUSTOMIZATION

THE EXPLOSIVE GROWTH OF THE GLOBAL MARKET AND THE rise of the bourgeois middle class are spawning a countertrend that is having an incredible influence on the mass-produced marketplace. While global brands have worked hard to develop corporate identities and products that are similar all over the world, the result is a proliferation of bland and generic products that don't take into account the individual needs of the consumer.

These brands are experiencing a backlash from consumers who don't want to be stereotyped. They no longer want what everyone else has. They don't want to keep up with the Joneses anymore. Instead, this increasingly self-confident group wants to be their own unique selves and to create a personal style driven by their individuality. They are not waiting for anyone else to tell them how to dress or how to be.

Here's a little perspective on how much things have changed. In the early 1900s, Henry Ford introduced our modern industrial world to the cost and time savings of mass production, boasting that customers could have any color they wanted, as long as it was black. A Model T was a Model T. Period. Take it or leave it.

This may have been acceptable in Ford's time, when mass production was a highly innovative idea, but that approach in today's marketplace is a recipe for disaster. In the new age, mass customization allows a product created for the masses to be "customized" to the point where each consumer feels it's all about him or her. And he or she is right, as products and services become increasingly tailored to each customer's needs, wants, tastes, lives, and desires.

Why is that so important? Psychologists tell us that through customization, consumers are on a quest to connect to their authentic selves while at the same time fulfilling their desire to stand out in a crowd and to be perceived as special. Companies are finding that, more and more, a commercial success as well as a healthy bottom line is dependent on making consumers feel that they are unique, or as Mini Cooper says, "Younique." So the challenge or the paradox becomes how to make something truly unique for the mass market. Let's take a look at a few companies that know how to do just that.

TRANSPORTATION: A Bicycle Built for *You*

MINI COOPER

We've come a long way from Henry Ford's production line. Today, the automotive industry is driving increased profits by offering the customer a menu of customizable options in many of their new vehicles. While the VW Beetle and the Chrysler PT Cruiser appeal to the consumer's nostalgic urges, the Mini celebrates the consumer's individuality.

Close to 95 percent of all Minis sold today are customized in one way or another. Demand is so high for these personalized vehicles that the waiting period is often 8 to 12 weeks.

In order to keep waiting customers happy, Mini Cooper created a "Where's My Baby" program online. Expectant owners can access the Web site anytime and track the progress of their very own cars. The site attracted more than twelve thousand registered users in the first few years, most of whom ended up naming their cars! Many of the new Mini owners actually send out "birth" announcements to their friends, heralding the arrival of their "Younique" offspring.

SCION XB

Forbes magazine reports that Toyota's Camry is the nation's best-selling car, particularly among baby boomers. You might not think there would be a problem with relying on this sizable demographic, but in a way there is. Toyota became concerned that the average age of its existing customers had risen to forty-eight years old. In an attempt to attract younger drivers, they set out to deliver a hip and customizable new vehicle for today's youth.

The Scion xB is marketed as "a cheap car with audacious accessories for the discriminating body piercer." Realizing that these kids like to customize their stuff, Toyota offers a menu of accessories that include illuminated cup holders, colored door-lock covers and steering wheels, even the color of the LED lights on the dashboard, that allow you to create your virtual vehicle online just the way *you* want it.

They revamped their distribution system with a new process that some are calling postponement. Unlike the Mini Cooper, Scions are not customized on the production line. Instead, they are shipped standard to American ports, where they are then customized to owners' specifications by special teams of mechanics at the docks.

It's the immediate gratification that really attracts the young drivers. Sure, you can wait several months for your Ford with your personal seat fabric selection. But Toyota has it set up so that as long as a standard model is in port, customers can get their special-option vehicle within a week of "designing" it online, or at the Toyota dealership.

It's nirvana for all those discriminating body piercers when they find out they can exercise their self-expression, fully loaded, for around $13,000.

SEROTTA BICYCLES

Imagine a bike that takes longer to build than a Mercedes. For true biking enthusiasts and serious competitive athletes, as well as celebrities like Robin Williams and John Kerry, nothing beats a custom-fitted bicycle.

Serotta, based in Saratoga Springs, New York, doesn't just custom design the bike, they custom fit it to the individual rider. Unlike the Scion, a Serotta bike is at the *top* end of the cost spectrum.

USA Today reports that a custom-made bike from Serotta can cost upward of $10,000. The bikes are expensive because each bike is built based on "personalized fittings," a method taught at the Serotta School of Cycling Ergonomics, where technicians learn the intricacies of melding a Serotta bike with its rider.

It seems a "fitting" is as much technical as it is psychological.

During a typical fitting, the customer is observed on a stationary bike as well as on his or her old bike. He or she is stretched out on a massage table and flexed on a yoga mat. Intricate measurements are taken with plumb bobs. Muscle movements are tracked with laser lights. It is equal parts art and science. And the resulting masterpiece is truly one of a kind.

With Serotta bicycles, we've moved way beyond "pick a color, any color." Two wheels, four wheels, or no wheels, if you can drive it or ride it, you should be able to find a way to customize it. MasterCraft boats recently created an online operation that allows potential customers to configure their own boats. The Minneapolis *Star Tribune* reports that almost 30 percent of MasterCraft's boat sales are custom orders. Internet access, coupled with the latest technology and advanced distribution models—and some truly revolutionary thinking—are transforming how we drive, ride, and even float.

CONSUMER ELECTRONICS:
Me, Myself, and iPod

Personal electronics are really starting to live up to their name. Even before TiVO hit the small screen, we began to have the ability to customize our own viewing and listening experiences in ways that are clearly of our own choosing.

VCRs allowed us to tape a regularly scheduled TV program and watch it when we wanted to. Today, there is an industry-wide trend to give the (remote) controls to consumers, and, as a result, manufacturers are pumping up the volume on profits.

IPOD

I heard a great expression recently: "Me, Myself, and iPod." For those who have one, the iPod is a status badge, a fashion statement, and oftentimes an obsession. "Poddicts" are members of a cult, albeit a cult of individuals (another paradox!), each lost in his or her own musical universe. Poddicts love the ability to sample individual songs from different artists, as well as the convenience of downloading music anytime they want—day or night. But most of all, they love being able to custom select and mix their music *their* way—and share it with their friends.

Apple leveraged a great design strategy—as well as modern psychology—when they developed the iPod. They also relied on brilliant marketing to get their message out. Their award-winning ads featured silhouetted models of all ages and ethnic backgrounds against bright backdrops that highlighted the psychology behind the concept. Anyone viewing those ads could immediately put him- or herself in the picture. The silhouetted personality is a music-loving Everyman—it leaves room for you to be you.

The success of the iPod has left other consumer electronics

companies scrambling to catch up. And it's done a nice job on Apple's stock price, which has more than tripled since the iPod was introduced.

CUSTOM RING TONES

Customized ring tones for cell phones have become a big business, with annual sales exceeding a billion dollars in the United States alone. The *Wall Street Journal* recently reported that in Japan Coca-Cola promotes its vending machines with wireless text offers, giving customers a free ring tone download featuring a Coke jingle with the purchase of each can of Coke. There was a 50 percent sales spike as a result of the ring tone promotion.

But why pay one to three dollars every time you want to download a new ring tone? XINGTONE allows you to make your own *real music* ring tones from any Mp3 or WAV file. Customization is as simple as choosing your favorite song—or favorite part of your favorite song. I hear a symphony.

NOKIA MEDALLION I

Jewelry has been a major component of personal expression throughout the ages. Nomadic tribes in Africa, American Indians, the harems of Persia, Victorian women in corsets, right down to today's youth with their multiple piercings and tattoos, all have utilized personal adornment as a billboard testament to their own individuality. Nokia found a way to leverage technology to create a modern version of the locket. The Medallion I was marketed as a unisex necklace when it was unveiled at the Consumer Electronics Show in Las Vegas in 2002.

Essentially, it's a device worn around the neck that you can send digital images to (via your PDA, cell phone, or computer) and that can hold up to eight images. This allows the sender of the images to change or customize the image in the necklace while it's being worn. You're in Alaska and your girlfriend is in Minnesota? Now you can send an image to her and share the experience in real time. Things not working out as well as you'd hoped? While breaking up is hard to do, the Medallion can help lesson the pain. New girlfriend? No problem. New picture . . . instantly!

FASHION: Just Do It . . . Yourself

In a certain sense, fashion has always been about showcasing your individuality. Today, however, the notion of personalizing fashion transcends monogrammed sweaters. What you wear and how you wear it say a lot about who you are—or aren't—and many fashion retailers are about to take that idea to a whole new level.

NIKE

Trend Central reports that customized sneakers have practically become a standard among teens and tweens. Nike has a new message for kids looking for the latest shoe design: Just do it . . . yourself! Nike iD is an online shopping experience where shoppers design their own shoes by choosing everything from the overall design to the fabric selection right down to the color of the famous Nike swoosh. You can even personalize the tongue with a custom word or phrase. Because most NikeiD shoes sell for more than $100, it's the kind of investment that encourages consumers to become vested in their personalized design.

Nike's taken their Nike iD online concept one step further with Nike iD Studio 255, located in Manhattan's *über*-hip NoLita neighborhood. Studio 255 is a gallerylike concept space that gives shoppers a hands-on custom design *experience,* complete with a design consultant and your very own design "pod." Initially limited to specially invited guests such as athletes and celebrities, the studio is now open for one-on-one design sessions to any interested sneaker fan who signs up on the Nike iD Web site.

LANDS' END

Lands' End was well ahead of the trend when they started selling custom-made pants on their Web site in 2001. By logging on to www.landsend.com, customers are able to type in measurements from height and weight to hips, thighs, and inseams. A computer program then analyzes that information and calculates the ideal dimensions of the pants, sending the necessary information to a manufacturing plant in Mexico. The finished product arrives at your door in two to four weeks, and the price tag is reasonable— around $60, plus shipping and handling.

When Lands' End launched this custom-fit venture, they estimated that custom-fit pants would account for approximately

10 percent of sales in that category. In less than a year, however, 40 percent of all chino and jean sales on the company's Web site was custom orders.

Many other retailers have followed suit. At their New York flagship store, Brooks Brothers utilizes a $75,000 body scanner that collects three hundred thousand data points of measurements in twelve seconds to custom-design men's suits. Trunk shows have always allowed the dapper gentleman to select his own fabric swatch and cuff length, but this new technology takes the custom concept to new heights.

Ralph Lauren offers a Create Your Own line of polo and oxford shirts, allowing customers to select from seventeen colors and six embroidered polo player logos. Even Target has a Target to a T program for ordering custom pants. Besides giving customers exactly what they want, the custom service helps reduce returns as well as the amount of unwanted merchandise in the warehouse. Profit margins are higher too, because custom fits carry a higher price tag.

YOUR SKIRT

Small boutiques are getting into the act, too. Finicky fashionistas can have their skirts their way when they shop at Your Skirt, a San Francisco boutique that specializes in custom-made skirts. Style options include pencil, A-line, bias, or mini—or invent your own. The staff at Your Skirt will sew it up just the way you want it. Customers . . . err . . . designers can chose from more than ninety designs and myriad fabric options, including leather, suede, silk, tweed, chino, and denim. All of this gives new meaning to the term *custom*ers.

HOME SEWING

When I was in high school, making your own clothes was a cool thing to do. I'll never forget the home economics class where I made a vinyl coat out of fake alligator-patterned material. I can assure you it was an original! No one had a coat quite like that one, and I doubt if anyone would have wanted one anyway. I, however, thought it was the coolest project in the class.

Today, home sewing is cool again. Once thought of as the domain of nerdy high school girls, being crafty is pretty trendy these days. *Time* magazine reported that the desire to make your own clothes and new technology that simplifies the sewing process have helped spawn a renewed interest in the domestic arts. Today, anyone with a sewing machine can create one-of-a-kind fashions. In fact, even teenage boys are getting in on the action. Skaters and snowboarders are knitting their own custom caps, designed to make a personal statement—as well as an apparent political statement in opposition to commercialism and homogeneity on the retail landscape.

But the main idea behind the trend is that style-conscious women who are bored by the cookie-cutter apparel sold at chain stores and discounters are buying their own sewing machines and opting to let their creative energies take over.

Many hip teens are now crafting and cutting their own patterns. They're much more interested in sewing as an expression of individuality than as a tradition. Designs are often adapted from vintage finds and then embellished by computers and photo images. New Web sites such as www.Craftster.org help aspiring designers find inspiration and also offer technical advice. *Time* reports that the Craftster.com Web site attracts 250,000 visitors a month.

3 CUSTOM COLOR

Cosmetic companies are joining the custom movement as well. One example of a small company making big waves in the industry is 3 Custom Color. They create custom shades of everything from lipstick to eye shadow to blush. You can send in anything as a sample to match: a fabric swatch, a discontinued shade of your favorite lipstick, a Pantone chip, and they'll ship back your custom-color tube of lipstick before you can say "lipstick on a pig." *And* they'll give you a choice of matte, gloss, shimmer, or sheer. The options have customers smacking their lips in satisfaction.

BANDSHADES

And then there's BandShades, a latex-free Band-Aid that helps protect your wounds without bringing attention to them. BandShades is the first cosmetic adhesive bandage offering several shades of skin tones to protect your wound. Choose from honey, caramel, bronze, cocoa, or mocha. Some clever marketer figured out that we're not all the same shade of Johnson & Johnson Band-Aid beige. Brilliant.

URBAN OUTFITTERS

In the past few years, massive consolidations of department stores have taken a toll on the retail environment, making a Macy's in Kansas City look a lot like a Burdines in Florida or a Marshall Fields in Minnesota. Hey, wait a minute. Macy's owns Burdine's and Marshall Fields now! No wonder everything is starting to look alike.

While department stores and chain operations have manifested incredible cost savings by taking the individuality out of their assortments, it's come at the expense of uniqueness. Regional personality has been wiped clean even while incredible efficiencies ensured by cookie-cutter sameness have added points to the bottom line. As departments stores go the way of the dinosaur, some specialty chains are having a field day by living up to their name, just by being special.

Urban Outfitters has done particularly well with a unique strategy that's actually a paradox. It's a new twist on the "loose-tight" properties outlined in the pages of *In Search of Excellence*. Basically, the company exerts rigid budget controls from the central office, but then gives each store a free reign when it comes to merchandising.

It's a little like two women wearing the same jacket, but in different ways. The stores may carry the same merchandise, but physically they all look different. An article about Urban Outfitters in *Forbes* magazine explains it this way: "No two stores are the same. Each store varies the displays, color schemes, cutout decorations, and soundtracks to give the illusion of being unique—even though the merchandise is essentially the same at each location." The formula has proven successful. Urban Outfitters continues to outperform most other fashion stores, and *Forbes* ranked it number 27 on their list of 200 Best Small Companies in 2004.

PFALTZGRAFF

For many people, their home is the ultimate expression of who they are. Where they live, how they decorate, and even how they entertain is a big part of their personal style expression. Casual dinnerware leader Pfaltzgraff has launched a new product line called pfz, a line of dinnerware that customers design to their own specifications through a new Web site. They've made it simple for the customer. There are fifteen different dinnerware items, including five plate designs, two mugs, three serving bowls, and five serving pieces that are fully customizable.

Aspiring designers can select colors, and mix and match them at will. They can embellish their tabletop further by adding a band in the style and color of their choice. They can also select a design pattern to accent the edges and/or centers of the plates. And they can further personalize the pieces with a monogram or customized back stamp.

The pfz program is targeted to young consumers who are comfortable using the Internet, and it appeals to those who prefer to showcase their own personal style as opposed to following the fashion trends of the moment. As Diana Vreeland said, "Fashion says 'me too.' Style 'only me.' " It appears that that sentiment is as appropriate for setting a table as it is for getting dressed in the morning.

FOOD: You Are What You Eat

You are what you eat, as the old adage says. As lifestyle trends proliferate, food has become another way to manifest individual preferences in unique and creative ways.

JONES SODA

Internet savvy and youth-conscious, Jones Soda has generated grassroots demand for its products and made customers prime participants in marketing the brand and keeping it fresh. Founder Peter van Stolk, a former ski instructor based in Seattle, set out to create something more than a beverage. He wanted to create a lifestyle, a fashion accessory. Van Stolk's philosophy was that his competitors had more money and he'd never be able to outspend them. Knowing he could never compete with the likes of Coke and Pepsi, he set out to leverage technology as a way to get to know his customers personally.

Jones Soda made digital technology the means to talk directly to their customers. For a minimum order of twelve bottles, customers can download a template, scan in their own photos, select a flavor, and e-mail it to the company. For $34.95 plus shipping and handling, customers can see themselves on a label of FuFu Berry or D'Peach Mode soda; The innovative marketing campaign has created a cult following of individuals, much as the iPod has.

BREWTOPIA

Trendwatching.com reports on a small brewing company in Australia that has taken the online customized order concept a step further. Brewtopia lets its customers design their very own full-strength premium lager online in just four minutes. You can customize the label with your logo, the name of your event, or a personal message and have it shipped directly to your home or business. With every purchase the customer gets an added bonus—a share in the brewery. As they say, "It's about owning the beer you drink." Now the trend has moved from customer-made to customer-owned, allowing the individual to be unique and a part of something at the same time. Paradox resolved.

M&M'S

Masterfoods USA, the division of Mars Inc. that owns M&M's, first launched customized colors in 1997, encouraging customers to select their own colors or combination of colors imprinted with the traditional M&M's logo. Today, M&M's offer twenty-one fashion shades of custom candy colors. They invite you to take a shot at designing your own blend. They want to help you make your message a little more colorful and leave a good taste in your mouth by printing your personal message on the M&M's candies. At the time of the launch, Bill Simmons, general manager of the Masterfoods business development team, told *Business-Week*, "We're using technology to give consumers the products they're after."

Customization has expanded their market and increased revenue, and it's created a lot of buzz as well. The personalized candies cost four times as much per ounce as the standard version, but many think it's worth it.

DOMINO'S PIZZA

Dominos has "glocalized" the art of pizza. The Ann Arbor–based global pizza chain has figured out how to remain consistently local by exercising central control and local flexibility—much as Urban Outfitters has done. Domino's successfully sells the same product in more than fifty countries—except it's not really the same product.

Instead, it's about theme and variation. The basics of crust, sauce, and cheese remain constant and are dictated by the corporate office. However, the toppings and combinations are customized by country and location. According to *Fast Company*, "They actually make more than 100 pies globally. India has paneer pizza, and Japan offers a specialized mayo-jaga pizza—potato, bacon, and mayonnaise." But no matter how you slice it, it's still a Domino's pizza.

COLD STONE CREAMERY

Cold Stone Creamery is the country's fastest growing ice cream franchise, opening an average of a store a day. They are reported to receive more than four thousand applications for franchises each month.

The company's been on a growth tear for the last five years, stirring demand for a product whose overall sales had been frozen solid for nearly a decade. Sales in ice cream shops around the country hadn't budged in ages, but Cold Stone rang up comp store sales of more than 50 percent in the last several years.

The secret to Cold Stone's success is customized cones. Cold Stone custom blends high-quality ice cream with your choice of "mix-ins" on the spot, in an entertaining atmosphere that allows you to watch. Customers choose from a variety of mix-in options, like Reese's Peanut Butter Cups, macadamia nuts, raspberries, brownies, and even occasional surprises such as chocolate-covered crickets (a special promotional tie-in with the reality TV show *Survivor* that landed them national exposure on the *Today* show). The customer selects a flavor, the type of cone, and the mix-ins. Employees then mix everything together, wielding metal ice cream spades on a polished granite stone that's refrigerated underneath, hence the name Cold Stone.

I remember my first visit to Steve's Ice Cream in Boston's Fanueil Hall back in the early nineties. Many credit Steve's with the invention of the concept. The lines in Quincy Market used to extend down the hall and out the door. Cold Stone managed to take this same concept to the masses, and today the proof is in the ice cream: If you don't want to be left out in the cold, figure out how to give your customers what they want, their way.

STARBUCKS

And what is Starbucks but the antithesis of "just a cup of coffee, please"? Not that long ago, a cup of coffee cost fifty cents, wherever you were. But it pretty much came to you one standard way. Then Starbucks came along and created a completely new way to mass customize the coffee experience.

Starbucks recently ran a series of ads called Customize Your Cup. One ad featured a photograph of a cup of coffee with a small handwritten bracketed note at the top that read "with room." Another ad in the series featured the same photograph with a handwritten notation that said "with vanilla." The tagline was Customize your cup, and the implication was clear.

This wasn't just a cup of coffee. It was *your* coffee, the way you wanted it. Tall, grande, vente? Choose from five different kinds of milk: whole, nonfat, half & half, organic, and soy. What blend of beans do you prefer: Sumatra, French, or Vietnamese? Decaf or regular? With foam or without? For here or to go? The options at Starbucks are actually pretty amazing. It's been documented that there are over more than nineteen thousand ways to order something to drink at Starbucks. The company has even printed a manual to teach customers how to effectively place an order from among the many options.

We've come a long way from "just a cup of coffee, please."

TOYS: It's a Me Me Me Me World

Many of today's parents have placed their kids smack dab in the center of the universe. I remember a print ad from *Los Angeles* magazine back in the early eighties for an upscale children's clothing store on Rodeo Drive. The ad featured a photo of an impeccably outfitted young girl snoozing in the backseat of a Rolls Royce, along with the headline BECAUSE YOUR CHILDREN ARE A REFLECTION OF YOU.

These days, it's not just clothes but *toys* that are being reflected.

BUILD-A-BEAR WORKSHOP

The U.S. toy industry has been in a rut for years, but a new mass customization concept is reviving at least one sector of the business. One of the most sought after mall tenants these days is a franchise called Build-A-Bear Workshop. It's basically a teddy bear factory where any child (or adult) can select, stuff, stitch, and wardrobe his or her very own stuffed animal.

Founder and chief executive Maxine Clark says, "Our interactive shopping experience, and the fact that we offer each guest a chance to personalize their stuffed animal, is the core difference between Build-A-Bear Workshop and a toy store." In essence, every product that they sell is one of a kind.

It's a delight for kids and "beary" profitable for investors as well. Aside from video games, Build-A-Bear is one of the few bright spots on an otherwise bleak toy landscape. After going public in

August 2004, their stock increased 85 percent in the first six months. Since then, they have consistently delivered quarters of double-digit comp sales increase, and they continue to expand and innovate. The long-term plan is to have 350 stores in the United States and Canada, and 350 additional stores internationally. They currently own or franchise stores in Great Britain, Australia, Japan, Denmark, and South Korea.

Build-A-Bear has found the honey pot and is sticking to its strategy to sell not just bears but a unique customized retail experience as well. Isn't it interesting that in a world where high-tech games and toys rule that the other hot trend is a bear with a heart?

MY TWINN

My Twinn is probably the ultimate narcissistic childhood experience a parent can offer a child. Customizing your very own teddy bear is one thing, but what about a doll that looks exactly like you?

Before you begin conjuring images of Jennifer Jason Leigh creepily morphing into Bridget Fonda's character in *Single White Female*, let me explain. My Twinn lets customers personalize a twenty-three-inch fully poseable doll to resemble any Joan, Dick, or Mary aged three to twelve, down to the smallest detail. Here's how it works. Customers select their doll's name, outfit, hair length, skin tone, eye color, and hair color. At no additional cost they can request special hand-painted details such as freckles, birthmarks, and moles. Mom or Dad fills out a personal profile and sends in a picture of the child. Special artisans choose facial features and style the doll's hair to create a remarkable resemblance.

Every child is an original. My Twinn promises to deliver a doll that is custom made to be a beautiful reflection of your special child. As they say, the real magic begins the second they meet, and before you know it, they're inseparable. Now if only your child would be as well behaved as their Twinn.

LEGO

If you build it they will come—at least that's what Lego figured out when they began an exciting new strategy designed to reconnect with their core customers on a personalized basis—brick by brick.

Lego Factory is a new initiative that lets fans decide what they'd like to build and then allows them to buy only the necessary bricks needed for their personalized design. Lego offers customers free access to specialized digital designer software that can be used on their own computers to develop original designs. Specialized factory workers handpick the Lego bricks that are imported from Europe and sort them into individual bags. The digital design software tells the packers exactly which bags they need to complete an order.

To date, customers have created more than seventy-seven thousand unique models, including renderings of the Danish Parliament and M. C. Escher's *Another World*. The concept also builds community among Lego fans as designs are shared on the company's Web site. Executives at the company foresee a day when sales of the custom building blocks will amount to 10 percent of their overall online sales. They're betting on the fact that if *you* design it, you'll want to build it, too—your way.

POSTAL STAMPS: Stamp of Approval

The Dutch postal system designed a way to create your very own personalized stamps, using a picture or photograph of your choice, valid on everything from postcards and letters to brochures and packages.

The process is facilitated by their TPG POST Web site. Customers simply access the "my stamp" application. After selecting a suitable decoration and uploading their photo of choice, they fill in their address and payment details, and a set of customized stamps is on its way. A minimum order of ten stamps costs about $14, a premium many are happy to pay.

Here in the United States, Stamps.com had $2.3 million in sales of personalized postage stamps as the sole vendor for last year's test for the U.S. Postal Service. (The test was shut down when Stamps.com failed to reject a handful of postage images sent to it, including photos of Theodore J. Kaczynski, the Unabomber, and Nicolae Ceausescue, former Romanian dictator.)

Now, however, the U.S. Postal Service has authorized a second round of tests with tightened screening controls. As a result, investors are again warming to the idea of personalized stamps. Many think the concept will stick the second time around.

Since the introduction of the Dutch online service, more than one million personalized stamps have been purchased. As you might guess, more than half of them have featured Dutch tikes. Just imagine: your pooch on your postcards, your new baby on birth announcements, your girlfriend on her Valentine's Day card, or your logo on your billing statement. It's all about you!

CONCLUSION

The pendulum has swung quite far from Henry Ford's Model T—and from the promise of owning one in any color as long as it's black. We've gone from demanding access to the same mass-produced things to wanting our mass-produced things to stand out from everyone else's mass-produced things. We are no longer content just to choose. We want to partake and to make.

Bottom line, we hate being stereotyped. Researchers long ago realized that they are no longer able to effectively profile customers just by demographics such as age, income level, education, or geographic location. Customers no longer fit into neat little categories. Customers will continue to demand a more personalized shopping environment and the ability to customize products to suit their individual needs.

Help your customer figure out how to be "Younique," and everyone wins.

CHAPTER 4
LUXURIOUS COMMODITIES

GOODNESS KNOWS, THE WORLD IS FULL OF BIG-TICKET items. From a six-figure Mercedes to a multimillion-dollar faux château, Manolo Blahnik shoes to shares in a charter jet, it's easy to spend a lot of money to buy the best. But the real art is in knowing how to treat yourself to affordable luxuries, even if they are just everyday objects.

In *Trading Up: The New American Luxury,* Michael Silverstein and Neil Fiske explore the phenomenon of the American consumer trading up to what they call a new kind of luxury. They document how America's upper middle class is choosing to buy better-quality goods, to become experts on the products they buy, and to look for and find emotional benefits in their purchases.

Put another way, Americans want to de-average their dreams, and they'll do it in many different ways. The authors estimate that millions of Americans have de-averaged by choosing to buy some $400 billion new luxury goods annually. Consumers are now willing to pay a premium price for luxury products and services such as Caldrea dishwashing liquid, Coach handbags, and Whole Foods artisan cheeses that possess higher levels of quality, taste, and aspiration—but are not so expensive as to be out of reach.

As a result, a genre of goods, many of which were once considered basics and now are viewed as small indulgences or luxuries, has emerged in the marketplace. A Starbucks coffee is anything but a basic. That is to say, it's far more than "just a cup of coffee." To many people it's a small indulgence, a little luxury they can easily treat themselves to during the day.

In my years of trend tracking and product development, I have been most fascinated by the companies that have found a way to reinvent an everyday commodity item in such a way that it brings extraordinary pleasure or meaning to our lives.

A commodity is a mass-produced, unspecialized product that is both useful or valued. A luxury is something that adds pleasure but isn't absolutely necessary. Surely then, a luxurious commodity qualifies as an enchanting paradox. It's all about taking a "need" and turning it into a "want." Let's take a look at some companies and products that are delivering on both ends of the luxury-commodity spectrum.

CALDREA

Most people would consider dishwashing liquid a commodity—a cleaning product that helps us take care of a task that isn't particularly pleasant. But not those women who know about Caldrea home cleaning products.

Caldrea is a line of luxurious, 100 percent natural aromatherapeutic dishwashing detergents, hand soaps, laundry detergents, window cleaners, and the like. The entire line helps turn a drudge into a dream, and women love the fresh aroma and the idea that there are no harsh chemicals to hurt your hands or pollute the environment. Some women I know even forgo using their dishwasher just so they can wash their dishes by hand.

This upscale product commands a premium price of around $8 a bottle, compared to Dawn and Joy that retail for $1 to $2 a bottle. But you won't find Caldrea products sitting on supermarket shelves next to those well-known commodities. Instead, women go out of their way to find the goods at upscale boutiques, furniture stores, and fashionable gift and home furnishings stores.

Caldrea products make a clean sweep of the commodity cleaning products world, injecting quality into the ingredients and luxury into the experience. It makes a mundane task a pleasure, if not an indulgence.

PHILLIPE STARCK SIPPY CUP

Phillipe Starck is a world-famous designer who has made a name for himself by redesigning everything from hotels and homes to baby bottles and garden trolls. When Target contracted with Starck for its infamous Starck Reality design project, no one knew quite what to expect.

One of the first items proposed by Phillipe was a sippy cup, a spillproof cup for children, that protected Mom's carpet and upholstery from becoming a mop for spilled juice and milk. Considered a necessity by the parents of any toddler, the sippy cup had a pretty standard design, which didn't usually include a pedestal.

Rather than just treat it as a commodity, Phillipe felt the item (and the child's experience) could be raised to a more glamorous level. The crystal-styled spillproof cup resembles a cut-glass miniature champagne bucket. The "goblet" is made of etched plastic featuring an X-pattern cut and a fetching yellow snap-on top. There are handles on either side (like a loving cup) so that baby can more easily grasp and hold it.

The designer once again managed to take an everyday product and elevate it to something truly special and different and, yes, even a little luxurious. For $3.49, it allowed babies and toddlers alike to live glamorously.

The cup became an icon for the buzz-worthy design project. After it was featured in a press kit that was distributed, I was surprised when I received numerous inquiries from countries around the world after the launch of the design project at the Milan IFF (International Furniture Fair) asking how they could buy a Starck sippy cup.

A seemingly ordinary item that was initially thought to be a "statement" item with marginal sales, it became an icon for the entire project. While sales weren't off the charts, the enormous buzz generated by this whimsical, yet functional, everyday object helped Target deliver some of its coveted "special sauce"—the

Starck sippy cup enhanced Target's ability to differentiate itself as a design leader. Today, if you're lucky, you can still find models offered for sale on eBay, at a price more in keeping with Waterford crystal.

WHIRLPOOL DUET

The term *white box commodity* was coined to describe the basic $800 washer and dryer pair that most homeowners of the eighties and nineties purchased for their new homes. These utilitarian tools were usually housed deep in the basement, and not much care or attention was given to their placement. Doing the laundry, like washing the dishes, was a chore.

Whirlpool changed all that a few years ago when they introduced their washer-and-dryer line called the Duet. In a few short months, the Duet became the fastest-selling appliance of its kind. In less than three years on the market, Duet captured a 20 percent share of sales in its category, despite its price of around $2,000 for the pair.

Called the "Ferrari of washing machines," these functional yet beautifully designed machines feature state-of-the-art technology such as a front-loading door so it's easy to load, and no agitator, so it's soft on clothes. It has an ultralarge capacity that can hold twenty-two towels in one washing. It's energy efficient— it actually uses 67 percent less water and 68 percent less energy than the competition, and it's quiet.

Deluxe features are all well and good, but ultimately consumers say they have an emotional attachment to the machines.

Their machines fulfill a desire and ultimately make a statement about the owner's self-worth. In 2005 the *New York Times* did a piece on the Duet and pointed out that it used to be the kitchen or the new spa bath that homeowners loved to show off to guests. Now, ironically, it's the luxury laundry room, complete with granite countertops and plasma screen TVs.

MICHAEL GRAVES TOILET BRUSH

A few years ago, *Newsweek* magazine did a feature article on how great design was changing the face of American consumerism. A Michael Graves toilet brush cleaner from Target was featured in a full-spread editorial. The article made the case that by applying great aesthetics and fine design to a commodity product, that product could be raised to a level of great desirability, as opposed to just need. This approach to product design and development became the cornerstone of the "Expect More. Pay Less." brand promise of *Tarzhay.*

It's ironic that the best-selling products and categories in the Michael Graves line at Target weren't the consumer electronics, the office products, the patio furniture ensembles, or the clocks and decorative accessories. The cleaning section, which included mops, buckets, sponges, toilet brushes, dustpans, and brooms, was one of the most productive runs (sales per square foot) in the merchandise assortment, followed closely by the garden tools. In other words, it was everyday items—commodities—that drove incremental sales in categories that were previously not thought of as important enough to apply great design principles to.

FOOD: Cheap Eats/Deluxe Dining

Ever since the birth of suburbia—when Dwight Eisenhower was president—Americans have counted on having their food fast and inexpensive. In fact, after a half century of fast-food living, our indomitable right to "hold the pickles" or "hold the lettuce" should probably be written into the U.S. Constitution.

Today, the conventional wisdom is being challenged as fast food and everyday items are being reinvented in a more upscale manner.

IN-N-OUT BURGER

By its very nature, fast food is considered a commodity. To most people, it's anything but luxurious. However, In-N-Out Burger, a family-owned and-operated burger chain based out of southern California, has built a fanatically loyal customer following and a very successful business by turning the basic burger and fries into a luxury worth making a pilgrimage for. They've built a phenomenal reputation on two beliefs that represent a paradox in the world of fast food and challenge the very nature of what fast food is.

First, they maintain that fast food should be made from scratch, and second, that the whims of the customer should be entertained. At In-N-Out Burger there are no freezers, microwaves, or heat lamps. The fries are cut by hand, on site, and the shakes are made from real ice cream. None of the food is ever frozen, no meal is prepared until the customer orders it, and nothing costs more than $2.50. Fans rave about the friendly service, the cleanliness of its facilities, and the simplicity of the menu, not to mention the taste of the cooked-to-order burgers and fresh-cut fries.

The *New York Times* reported that In-N-Out Burger is where "Southern California's rich and famous go when they crave the pleasure of a burger and fries." I'm not sure how many Hollywood types hang out at Burger King or McDonald's! Each year at its famous "after-Oscar" party, *Vanity Fair* magazine offers In-N-Out Burgers to hungry stars such as burger fan Bill Murray.

HOT CHOCOLATE

Hot chocolate has come a long way from Swiss Miss and Carnation Instant. The comforting steaming beverage of childhood winter nights has gotten a sexy makeover from the biggest names in the hot-drink business. And the public is drinking it up.

Chocolate was once consumed by the Aztecs and other native tribes as part of a ritual. An infusion of cocoa extract and various spices and chile peppers were once considered food for the gods. The emperor Montezuma apparently drank fifty goblets daily.

Cortez brought back the cocoa concoction to Spain, where monks sweetened the dark delight with sugar and vanilla. Initially the drink was a highly guarded secret kept sacred by the monks, but the idea spread throughout Europe and was eventually established as a drink fit for royals.

Today's luxurious versions are once again a gourmand's delight. Godiva offers a deliciously steamy sacred treat called Hot Chocolixir at select Godiva boutiques, and the urban bakery Au Bon Pain began offering a trio of high-end cocoa drinks called Choco Bon Loco. These thick, luxurious, deliciously rich delights are practically desserts—a far cry from the watery packaged concoctions that resemble commodities.

TEAVANA

Tea has been around in one form or another for centuries. Long a staple of European and Asian diets, tea is now catching on in the United States. While teahouses are not yet as ubiquitous as the coffee house, one Atlanta-based company is trying to change all that. Teavana is a fast-growing specialty teahouse and retailer that virtually pioneered the mall-based teahouse concept.

The United States tea industry is expected to grow between 30 and 40 percent from 2005 to 2010, according to the Tea Association of the United States of America, Inc. And much of that business is expected to be in upscale specialty teas and accessories along the lines of what Teavana sells.

Specializing in loose teas that have more healthful benefits than the bagged commodity teas sold in most supermarkets, Teavana also sells tea accessories from Japanese cast-iron teapots to tea measures. Teavana's loose teas range from $3 for two ounces of Black Currant to $25 for two ounces of Monkey Picked Oolong.

Wait a minute. Monkey Picked Oolong? Of course! Remember, we're talking rare and luxurious here. Monkey Picked Oolong is a very rare, light-tasting tea from a mountainous region of China. Legends say Buddhist monks once dispatched trained monkeys to pick the leaves from the tops of the wild tea trees growing in the region.

People in the United States are already drinking better coffee, more prestigious vintages of wines, and more high-end luxury spirits. You don't have to be able to read tea leaves to see that it might be profitable to raise the taste level of tea drinkers and introduce them to a luxury tea experience. Who knows, perhaps they'll even succeed in converting some die-hard java addicts to the Zen approach to quenching thirst.

ANNIE'S MAC & CHEESE

Growing up, Kraft's Deluxe Macaroni and Cheese Dinner used to be a real treat for lunch. I loved it so much that my mom used to tease me that I was going to turn yellow from eating it so often. While Kraft still owns the lion's share of the macaroni-and-cheese market, enterprising purveyors of gourmet experiences are building profitable niche businesses by revamping a food staple into a luxurious treat.

Annie Withey is one that has taken a different approach to every schoolkids' lunch staple. Her mac and cheese appeals to consumers who are less price sensitive and willing to pay more to feel good about what they eat. She insists on all-natural organic cheddar and uses petite shells to differentiate her product from the commodity versions that use the classic elbow-shaped macaroni. She charges about 30 percent more than Kraft, and while her share of the U.S. mac-and-cheese market may be only 3 percent, her forty-five-person company posted revenues of $34 million for the 2004 fiscal year. That has some food companies turning green with envy.

TRAVEL: King of the Road

People want cheap, but they still want good. From airlines to hotels to just about every other aspect of the travel business, consumer-savvy businesses are enhancing their cachet in ways that allow consumers to hang on to their cash.

LUFTHANSA

The same airlines that are working their way through bankruptcy all maintain frequent-flier lounges. The Delta Crown Room, Northwest World Perks Lounge, and the Admiral's Club were originally formed to offer valuable frequent-flier customers an exclusive oasis in which to relax while waiting for connections or during weather delays. For a yearly membership fee (the cost of which has increased dramatically over the years), members were treated to "free" drinks and snacks, "complimentary" Internet connections, and comfortable seating. Once a novelty and an upscale oasis, the financial plight of the airline industry began to take its toll on the service level and appearance of these clubs, not to mention their amenities. Many lounges are disappearing all together from the nonhub airports.

Lufthansa is going countertrend. In 2005, they opened the

first terminal in the world where passengers are treated like VIPs everywhere they go. That's because the entire terminal is really a luxurious frequent-flier lounge. Located within Frankfurt Airport, the terminal caters to just 350 travelers daily. Each one is met by a personal assistant who handles all of the details, from baggage check-in to seat assignments. Those pampered few then get to wait in an opulent lounge that has overstuffed Italian leather chairs, a linen-tablecloth restaurant, and a cigar area with a selection of fifteen high-end whiskeys. Offices are available for high-level meetings, and the bathrooms are as elegant as those found in a five-star hotel. Immediately prior to departure, fliers are whisked to their plane in a Mercedes or a Porsche. Apparently, the idea is taking flight, as Lufthansa is planning a similar terminal in Munich and perhaps other airports as well.

GOURMET GAS STATIONS

As American gas stations become more automated and self-service, Japan's sixth-largest gas station chain, Jomo, is heading in the opposite direction. By adding elements of luxury, Japanese gas stations are enticing patrons to linger longer at the pumps and spend more money while they're parked.

Jomo calls the new approach Value Style, but from a service perspective, it falls beautifully into the luxurious commodities category. The company hired a leading Tokyo restaurant designer who introduced not only improved pumps but also comfortable cafés, kiddie areas, and even massage chairs.

Even more fun, they introduced the "car-wash dance," which includes two men in blue suits gyrating around your vehicle, wielding hoses through the air like samurai swords. As they towel dry the car, their movements are choreographed into a dance that many find entertaining enough to elicit spontaneous applause and exorbitant tips.

While the concept is basically an extension of Japan's commitment to quality service, it's also an adaptation of the Experience Economy. It might even be an antidote to road rage.

Not to be shut out of the fast lane, some gas stations here in the United States are taking a similar approach. Tiger Fuel is a Virginia convenience chain that offers more than cheap gas-and-go self-service. The *New York Times* reports that "it's an unlikely culinary revolution, but Slim Jims are making way for sushi as convenience stores transform themselves with upscale eats and shed their image as junk food pit stops."

With rising fuel prices, it's getting harder to get customers in the door based on perceived value. Even so, a good price on gas might attract people to stop once a week (at most) to fill up their tank. As the article points out, however, "great coffee, brick-oven pizza, and gelato could pull them in daily."

After all, it's all about the *journey,* not the destination. The concept of gas station luxury opens up innumerable options. For example, ExxonMobil's hot beverages manager has even created a new position at its stores—brew master.

THE PARKING SPOT

Two midwestern businessmen have come up with the idea of positioning the lowly off-site airport parking lot as something more than a pain-in-the-neck cost saver. The Parking Spot is a five-year-old company that owns and operates parking lots in more than ten cities around the country, including Dallas, Atlanta, Los Angeles, and Orlando. Their distinctive bright yellow shuttle busses are adorned with bold, black "ink" spots that make their service easy to identify. Besides selling you a place to park, the Parking Spot offers additional small indulgences such as free newspapers, bottled water, a frequent-parker loyalty program, and a reservations system that takes away a lot of the hassle of parking outside the airport grounds just to save a few dollars.

The easy-to-spot buses run every five to seven minutes. The drivers are friendly and knowledgeable, and even help you with luggage. For many frequent travelers, the Parking Spot hits the spot. It's more than a place to park a car. It's a fun alternative to the boring airport parking experience.

AIRSTREAM'S SKY DECK

For years, the middle class found RV travel to be an economical way to see the country. Today, scores of retirees choose to invest in an RV as a way to transform themselves into snowbirds, at least part time, without having to invest in real estate and pay taxes until they die.

Airstream had a different market in mind when they designed their Airstream SkyDeck, an upscale convertible RV that features a rooftop lounge, complete with an entertainment center, wet bar, barbeque, and snazzy beach umbrellas. For a mere $262,000, ultraluxe road warriors can enjoy a panoramic view from their ultimate party pad. Turns out that the latest status symbol in the RV park is cocktail parties on the top deck. You rise to the occasion by taking an elegant hardwood staircase inside the coach up to the roof, and the open-air patio seats at least fifteen people. The RV-park party circuit will never be the same.

HOTELS: CHEAP-CHIC SLEEP

If you're the type of on-the-go traveler who'd rather skip the RV and settle for a hotel room, there's hope. In the past, low-cost accommodations meant faceless, unmanned bed factories, while deluxe often meant too much gilt and too much money. Recognizing this gap in the market, a new breed of hoteliers is striving for high design at a low cost.

Here in the United States, the InterContinental Hotels Group recently introduced Hotel Indigo, an intriguing hotel that delivers "high peace and renewal" to people who are tired of mundane cookie-cutter hotels. Hotel Indigo's interior styling evokes a sense of home and welcome. The hotel's rooms feature plush bedding, wooden floors with area rugs, spa-inspired bathrooms, cool outdoor colors, and important details that matter to discerning travelers, such as free wireless Internet access. All this for less than $110 per night.

Starwood Hotels has also announced that they're looking to

reach new heights by going the cheap-chic route with their new brand aloft. Conceived by the team behind the successful W hotels, aloft will feature urban-inspired, loftlike guest rooms, a comfortable lounge scene, and landscaped outdoor spaces for socializing day and night, all at an affordable room rate. Special amenities like Mp3 docking stations, flat-panel TVs, and of course, free wireless Internet are included in the room price.

In the United Kingdom, the trend is really taking off. At Zetter in London, £125 will get you original mid-twentieth-century furniture, Hansgrohe Raindance walk-in showers, and, with a swipe of your key card in the carousel vending machine, your choice of chilled champagne charged directly to your room.

Singapore's Hotel 1929 has tiny rooms stuffed with design classics at super-low rates. Hamburg's haven of cheap chic and deluxe design is Kai Hollman's 25 Hours Hotel, where you get Flos lamps, Brionvega TVs, and exposed concrete. Travelodge, the United Kingdom's fastest growing hotel brand, is opening deluxe budget hotels in both the UK and Spain with smart interiors courtesy of the Conran Design Group. Think flat-screen TVs, wood and leather interiors, and a twenty-four hour larder on each floor.

But the cheapest of chic will ultimately be EasyHotel, currently open for business in London and Basel. The fiberglass rooms are prebuilt in Finland and are all sci-fi functionality. They have no phone or TV, but you can book rates as low as $20 per night if you book in advance. Cheap, clean, and chic, with lots of dough left over to buy that pair of Manolos or that Hermès scarf you have your heart set on. Rest assured, your design sensibilities will be satisfied and your pocketbook won't be empty.

FASHION: The Emperor's New Clothes

How did T-shirts go from being a commodity item—worn but never seen—to an exalted fashion icon? How did sweat suits become chic? And why is there bling now on everything from bras to Mp3 players?

In the world of fashion, it was merely a matter of time before basic essentials morphed into luxuries.

DENIM: DISTRESSED DELUXE

In the summer of 2005, the *New York Times* asked a rhetorical question: WHO PAYS $600 FOR JEANS? Turns out a lot of people will pay a lot of money for an item that was once was called dungarees and considered more appropriate to wear on a construction sight with steel-toe work boots than at a fashion premier with a pair of Jimmy Choo stilettos.

The work uniform invented by Levi Strauss during the gold rush era is now priced at figures resembling the price of gold. For the past several years, high-priced designer denim and other luxury versions of the working class staple have been the fastest growing category of the bottoms business.

Guy Trebay reported that "jeans with price tags of $200 plus are now everywhere, the retail equivalent of dandelions after spring rain." Prices can range right up there with the cost of a new fully loaded computer or a diamond bezel–studded watch. That's a lot of money to pay for a pair of jeans that requires approximately three yards of fabric. And there's a lot of irony in the fact that they are often ripped, torn, distressed, sandblasted—intentionally made to look old, used, and abused.

Robert Burke, fashion director of Bergdorf Goodman at the time, was interviewed for the story in the *New York Times* and was quoted as saying, "Now that premium is a fashion staple, everyone is wondering one thing: How high is high?" It seems that the sky is the limit when it comes to what certain people are willing to pay for the right pair of jeans.

JUICY COUTURE: SUPREME SWEAT

The same idea holds true for sweat suits. Sweat suits used to be worn for hanging out and for working out, period. The only people who'd dare to be caught in public wearing them were aspiring Rockys. They were usually 100 percent cotton, machine washable, and no one cared, really, if they were ripped, torn, or sweated in.

Not so anymore. Today, Juicy Couture has raised the art of sweat suit design to a new fashion high. They've essentially reinvented the sweat suit in cashmere, terry cloth, fleece, and velour in a rainbow of fashion colors, and in the process they have positioned themselves as "the uniform of aspiring actresses," according to Alex Kuczynski in the *New York Times*.

Worn by teenagers and aging baby boomers both, Juicy

appeals to the new suburban female, who represents a "muddle of paradoxes," according to Kucznynski. She profiles the customer as follows: "She wants to please like a child and [attract attention] like a woman. . . . She yearns for tradition yet admits she must purchase it. She wants to be both a preppy, ready to hit the links with Dad, and a punk rocker sneering in her spray-painted oxford shirt. She wants to show off her physique, yet eat candy hearts and bonbons like a child." Until that paradox is resolved, both Lolita and her mother are going to be wearing Juicy.

CHRISTIAN DIOR CONTACT LENSES: EYE CLASS

For many of us nearsighted fashion lovers, contact lenses are a necessity in life. The investment we make in purchasing prescription contact lenses helps us to see better and look better. Lenses are to eyes what braces are to teeth.

However, Christian Dior, the famous haute couture fashion house, has found a way to look at this market a little differently. Designer John Galliano has come up with two new sets of contact lenses for Dior Eyes that will do for eyes what Dior handbags and cosmetics do for your wardrobe. Dior has found a way to enhance and intensify the eye's appearance without changing its natural color.

A unique design circles the iris with either a golden or a black ring and contains a miniature CD logo. The ring design dramatizes the eyes, and the logo helps identify whether the lens is in the correct way. The lenses are on limited sale in London; they are available in a silver box with a sliding case and mirror for £79, or in a prêt-à-porter silver box for slightly less. Each pair lasts a maximum of two months.

Designers have long been accustomed to putting their logos on everything from jeans to handbags to perfume to connote luxury and command extremely high prices. Dior's concept is sure to make a spectacle of the wearer in a unique and differentiated manner.

OTHER LITTLE LUXURIES

A clever marketer will explore *all* of their product offerings—in order to turn a "need" into a "want" (or "desire").

SWAROVSKI IPOD: ICE IS NICE

The iPod has risen to the status of a cult object. Poddicts are now finding new ways to make the ubiquitous cutie even cuter. Swarovski, the venerable crystal fashion house, is producing a special version of the iPod Mini and the iPod Shuffle with some serious bling. The glitzy model is decorated with a thousand crystals (one for each of the one thousand songs it can store). These one-of-a-kind crystal digital music players are carefully handcrafted with strategically placed crystals from front to back.

The crystallized iPods sell for more than four times the cost of an unmodified version. Reviews are mixed. One blogger commented, "Why not just put a sign on yourself saying, 'Rob me, please'?" But others think the "ice is nice" and that the iPods are "gorgeous babies."

The Eglu by Omlet

OMLET HEN HOUSES: CHEAP-CHIC CHICK

You've probably never thought about it, but if you were a hen, where would you want to live? A British based company called Omlet has answered that question for today's discriminating poultry citizens, as well as for the growing masses of urban farmers.

Designers have created a colorful and clever new design to make it easy for consumers to grow and produce their own organic eggs and chickens. The Eglu is to lucky chickens what a high-priced urban loft is to upscale yuppies. The colorful pods (available in red, orange, pink, grass green, and blue) come complete with organically reared and fully vaccinated female chickens. Which means no cockadoodledoo to disturb your neighbors.

Priced at around $700, it's an investment in starting the day right. The special hen kit is aimed at first-time chicken owners, families, and eco-savvy urban hipsters and suburban gardeners. As the company says on its Web site: "We wanted it to be as easy as looking after a goldfish but more rewarding than owning a dog. Keeping a couple of chickens in your garden doesn't require a large investment of money or time, but you do get fantastic tasting eggs and a good feeling inside."

Voilà. Your chickens have a luxurious home, and you get cheap fresh organic eggs for morning breakfast. Now that's something to crow about!

FUNERAL URNS: DESIGNER DEATH

Rest assured (in eternal peace) knowing that when the time comes you can leave this world in a deluxe manner without worrying that your family will have to break the bank to send you out in style. The Renaissance Urn Company offers upscale designer cremation vessels to transport your ashes in style to your final resting spot.

In 2004, Mary and Bob Hickey began marketing fancy, handmade, artistic cremation vessels up and down the California coast. They started out selling beautifully designed ceramic urns; but when they found out that half of the people taking away cremains used small plastic boxes, they created sleek, silk-cushioned covers for the impersonal plastic boxes that are normally handed to grieving family members at the funeral home (think Kate Spade-esque slipcovers).

As they dug deeper, their research told them there was even

more life in the cremation business. About one in four people who died in the United States in 2001 was cremated, a percentage that's expected to climb to more than one in three by the year 2010. They also discovered that as more and more people retire to places far from their longtime homesteads and die there, more cremated remains need to be transported back home for scattering or burial.

Renaissance silk-covered urns go for about $80, and they're selling like hotcakes. Turns out its not just aesthetics driving sales power. The business got an unexpected boost post 9/11 as security concerns around air travel intensified. The Hickeys discovered that most conventional urns are made of metal- or lead-lined ceramic. Because these urns are opaque to X-ray equipment, they had to be placed in the checked luggage, destined for the baggage-claim carousel.

Guess what? Most people don't like to put Mom or Dad through the carousel with all the other baggage because they are afraid they'll get lost and end up who knows where. In April 2005, the Transportation Security Administration began advising funeral homes that customers traveling by plane with cremains must use an urn that can be x-rayed if they want to take it as a carry-on item. As a result, designer funeral urns were born. Aren't you just dying for one?

CONCLUSION

Call it cheap chic, luxurious commodities, or Masstige, making the everyday object into an object of desire is a formula that has application for every industry and every product or service. Martha Stewart would say, "It's a good thing." And the Church Lady? "Isn't that special?" What had these manufacturers figured out that others hadn't? They figured out how to make the mundane beautiful and the basic deluxe.

CHAPTER 5
LESS IS MORE

AMERICANS ARE INFATUATED WITH *BIG*. WE LOVE TO DRIVE Big cars, live in Big homes, eat Big portions, shop at Big box stores and Bigger-than-ever malls. We are a "Supersize me" nation, trained to believe that more is better. The ramifications are amazing.

Automotive makers have had to reengineer the cup holders in their cars and mini vans to be able to accommodate all those Big Gulp drinks we buy at convenience stores and fast-food outlets. Malls have gotten so Big that people visit them for vacations and park their RVs in the lots for an entire weekend so that they can take it all in. The typical American family has gotten progressively smaller over the years; our homes have gotten progressively Bigger. Today, the average single-family home is twenty-three hundred square feet, compared to fourteen hundred in 1970. The new plasma televisions in our homes have screens so Big that they often take up an entire wall in a family room. No need to buy great art anymore. Our waistlines are expanding too, and is it any wonder with the size of portions that food companies and restaurants offer? We have muffins as Big as houses, steaks that look like half a side of beef, and mugs of coffee that can hold an entire pot.

Thankfully, however, not everyone is convinced that bigger is better, or that more is indeed more. There's a backlash to this Big trend, and growing numbers of consumers are embracing the mantra of the countertrend: less is more. Maybe perfection isn't all that it's cracked up to be, and we really don't need a house the size of a fortress when we're only a family of three. Let's take a look at some companies that are tapping into the "simple is better" countertrend and finding out that you don't need to go Big to make Big bucks.

SMALLER IS BETTER

SCHONBEK CHANDELIERS: TINY, NOT TITANIC

I love looking through home magazines. While leafing through the pages of *Architectural Digest* one day, I happened upon an ad titled "The Trend to Tiny." It struck me as paradoxical. Here I was looking at glittering monuments to wealth and power, mansions staffed by servants, decorated by some of the biggest designer names in the business, and someone was promoting "Tiny instead of titanic. Playful rather than palatial. More darling than dazzling."

And I loved it. It pushed my magic button. It was different

and somehow more real. It intrigued me to the point that I had to keep reading, even though I didn't have a mansion to decorate.

Schonbek Worldwide Lighting, Ltd, has been making elegant crystal chandeliers since 1870. They've made their share of glittering and glorious ballroom-size pieces over the years. In keeping with the "less is more trend," they've gone from big and beautiful to tiny and tantalizing. Today, their ads in *Architectural Digest* feature their miniature crystal chandeliers, measuring no more than twelve or fourteen inches in width.

Described as "jewel-like" (which implies precious to me), the ad promotes these gems as a perfect way to glorify small rooms (in big houses) and to serve as exclamation points in subspaces in too-vast great rooms. The Schonbek Web site promotes the tiny chandelier as perfect for dainty bedrooms, elegant bathrooms, and intimate spaces. They market them as "coy little chandeliers for anywhere and everywhere, just for fun."

By thinking big about small, Schonbek virtually created an entirely new product category that they now own. They were smart enough to recognize a countertrend when they saw one. By going the other direction and celebrating small, they've made a big impact on their business. Their tagline says it all: "Big is beautiful. But tiny is tempting. Just make sure it's a Schonbek."

THE NOT-SO-BIG HOUSE: MINIMAL SQUARE FOOTAGE/ MAXIMUM STYLE

The name McMansion suggests something huge and monolithic; something too big. That is, too big for their lots, for their neighborhoods, and for the number of people who actually live in them. The houses offer every option money can buy, including seldom-used formal dining rooms, media rooms the size of your old local theater, pantries the size of ballrooms for nonexistent butlers, and laundry rooms that rival most day spas—not to mention three- and four-car garages and even separate showers for the dog. And McMansions just keep getting bigger and bigger, despite our shrinking family units.

While owning the biggest house in the neighborhood may have been the goal of baby boomers in their acquiring years, today's boomers are often opting for smaller and simpler. Finally, some people are saying "enough already." Sarah Susanka is the

Minnesota architect who started a countertrend to McMansions. Her 1998 best-selling book *The Not So Big House* takes a fresh look at how many people want to live now.

Susanka argues the importance of scale and livability. In the Duomo in Florence, for example, or at the Lincoln Memorial, you're supposed to be awed and feel insignificant in the bigger scheme of things, but not in your own home. With a master suite the size of a corporate boardroom, how cozy or intimate can you get?

Susanka explores how small spaces can be put to ingenious uses and a house can be made to feel like a home again. Her mini movement makes a case for downsizing and simplifying. She points out that just because you decide to downsize your square footage doesn't mean you have to downsize your dreams.

I'm sure homes will continue to get bigger and bigger, and today's McMansions will eventually become yesterday's cottages. But more and more, people who care about good design, the environment, and experiences versus "things" will opt out of the new house market all together. Instead, they'll chose to remodel smaller, older, not-so-big-homes; homes that come with a history and a patina that all the faux finishing in the world couldn't emulate.

LIFESTYLE SHOPPING CENTERS: "LESS IS MORE" IS HERE TO STAY

Shopping malls are getting bigger and smaller at the same time. The Mall of America has been a huge success. Situated on more than seventy-eight acres, it features more than four hundred shops and restaurants under one roof, along with an aquarium, a wedding chapel, a twenty-screen movie theater, and a complete theme park. The parking garage is humongous, with spaces for thirteen thousand cars. You can get a lot of exercise there in a day, walking from your car to the mall, or from one anchor store to the next. And while that's good for our ever-expanding waistlines, many consumers don't have the time it takes to shop that way.

The countertrend to bigger and bigger malls is what shopping center developers are calling lifestyle centers. They're small, convenient, open-air complexes laid out to evoke the small-town shopping districts of an earlier generation (sounds like "Everything old is new again" doesn't it?). They feature street-side parking and open-air plazas with fountains, fieldstone fireplaces, and cozy garden seating.

Ironically, lifestyle centers are meant to be reminiscent of the very thing that the covered shopping malls originally put out of business: downtown Main Street U.S.A. Dotted with cafés and sprinkled with street performers who sing, dance and juggle, the pedestrian streets are vibrant and lively. The store mix is more diverse than in a typical mall, featuring local independent boutiques and unusual retail concepts like pet spas. Department stores and other Big Box venues are glaringly absent.

Unlike the King of Prussia Mall and the Mall of America that seem to turn their backs on their surroundings and concentrate activity in and on themselves, lifestyle centers gesture toward the environment and the real world. They convey a sense of being out and about in the world. Developers hope that by emphasizing convenience and entertainment and making the centers smaller and more lifestyle oriented, centers will lure shoppers who will come more often and stay longer. According to the International Council of Shopping Centers, there are already more than 120 lifestyle centers in the United States—with many more on the drawing boards. It seems that "less is more" is here to stay.

MINI STORE FORMATS: BIG STORES GO SMALL TO GROW BIG

Faced with dwindling sales and sagging market share, many supermarkets are going small to combat the big superstores that have moved into their territories. Instead of going head to head and building supermarkets as big as parking lots, many are reversing direction and going small to grow bigger.

The old one-stop shop idea works for some, but not every consumer has the kind of time it takes to park, navigate, and wait in line to check out of the superstore behemoths. Many consumers prefer a more intimate, finely tuned assortment that caters to their specific lifestyles and tastes.

Harrods, the enormous London department store, has recently announced that it will test a convenience concept called Harrods 102. The first unit opened in 2005 just opposite the giant Knightsbridge flagship. Harrods 102 features many of the same specialty foods that are sold in the famed food halls across the street. But this location is not only smaller, it's more convenient. In addition to convenience-packaged gourmet take-out foods, more traditional convenience foods, such as coffee and tea, will also be offered. The store's hours of business will provide greater access than the traditional department store hours—open from seven to eleven (sound vaguely familiar?).

Wal-Mart has developed a strategy to grow bigger with smaller units. While their Sam's Club concept satisfies the Big Box end of the spectrum, their Neighborhood Market stores are smaller, and more convenient, and enable them to expand their presence in smaller towns and locales where a bigger "footprint" may not fit or be cost efficient.

Fewer SKUs, smaller footprints, less hassle. More fun, more service, greater convenience. For some, less is indeed more. Retailers are discovering that that formula equals more frequent visits, along with lower overhead and higher sales. For many it's not only a simple strategy; it's a winning one.

PYGMY MAGAZINE: A LITTLE MAGAZINE WITH A BIG PUNCH

I remember anxiously awaiting the August issue of *Seventeen* magazine when I was in high school. It was always a monster issue, packed with back-to-school fashions, and I wanted them all. Years later, once I'd landed in the fashion business, it was the first fall issue of *Vogue* that I coveted. Each season the number of pages would increase, the tomes would get heavier and heavier, the ads glossier and glitzier. More was more, and more was good.

In true trend/countertrend fashion, there's now a "less is more" fashion magazine. Condé Nast, which is known for producing large, lush magazines in the United States, is doing exactly the opposite in Europe. The well-known publisher of such fashion mastheads as *GQ, Vogue,* and *Glamour* has downsized both the size and the content of the fashion magazine *British Glamour* to pocket size. The *New York Times* reports that the unlikely tactic is a hit in Britain, where the magazine is now "the best-selling monthly magazine" in the land, with a total circulation of more than six hundred thousand—about one hundred fifty thousand more than British *Cosmo,* owned by rival publisher Hearst Magazines.

Cool News commented that when the mini version of *British Glamour* was introduced, the *Cosmo* crowd dismissed it as "pygmy," and Hearst president Cathleen P. Black said she'd squish it like "a little armadillo in the road."

Nevertheless, the armadillo is alive and well and kicking butt. Jonathan Newhouse, the mastermind behind the pocket-size coup, said it wasn't just size that made the difference. A better reader experience has a lot to do with it. The new concept relies less on paid advertisements and more on increased newsstand sales. The reader gets all the fashion, beauty, and lifestyle information they can digest, without an overabundance of ads.

A recent review on Amazon.com by a reader described the magazine this way: "The British version is more fashionable than its American counterpart. It's trendier, wittier, and gets straight to the point. Plus it's a great size that makes it easy and fun to carry around." Another reader expounds: "It immediately caught my eye due to its clever size. It's a smidge larger than a *TV Guide,* just the right size to pack in my beach bag or sneak into my briefcase."

Newhouse, an American, has big ambitions for this small magazine. Plans to roll out the concept into markets that seem small on the map but are significant when put together are in the works. By the end of the decade, Newhouse anticipates mini-size versions of *Glamour* in Greece, Poland, South Africa, and Hungary, to name but a few. Revenues are expected to grow to more than a billion dollars, all generated without huge revenues from advertisers.

More content, fewer ads. Small size, big delight, and big success.

"LESS IS MORE": Mini Is Mighty

Homes continue to get bigger and bigger, Hummers and SUVs rule the road, and Supersize portions make a star out of an unknown producer. Americans are on a roll when it comes to big, but in true trend/countertrend fashion, they also love mini.

Not since the miniskirt has America been so fixated on the barely there. The Mini Cooper automobile makes cute look clever. The iPod goes from small to mini to nano. Micro breweries grow their share of the beer drinking market, and mini spas for the maxi stressed pop up everywhere. Conferences feature mini workshops and colleges offer mini credits. Mini Oreos and mini pizzas are featured at the grocery store. Tapas restaurants serve mini portions to hungry diners worldwide. Health food stores offer mini massages and hotels advertise mini vacations for the time pressed. Even newspapers such as the *Washington Post* are shrinking from broadsheet to tabloid size. What's going on here anyway?

It seems that these days, if you're thinking big, you've also got to be thinking small. So, think about what you can shrink. Small implies simplicity. In my book *The Trendmaster's Guide*, K is for Keep it Simple. I could have just as easily said Keep it Profitable. The retailer simply repackages it into bite-size portions, and the consumer happily pays a higher price for the convenience and the novelty.

LESS COMPLEXITY: Simply Better

Linda Tischler, in an article for *Fast Company* magazine titled "The Beauty of Simplicity," summed up the small idea brilliantly: "Sure, technology has given us many wonderful things—satellite phones, plasma TVs, and online tickets to Machu Picchu. But way too much tech is way too complex. Making it simple is the next big thing."

Now that's something that I can relate to. The last time I went to purchase a new cell phone, I was overwhelmed with options. I just wanted one like my old one. Instead I was shown cell phones that took pictures, made movies, connected to the Internet, and could serve as a mini TV, to name just a few extraneous features I wasn't the least bit interested in.

Granted, there is an elite cohort of techno-geeks who want it all—every feature, every gadget, an option menu a mile long. But most consumers abhor complexity in their gadgets and readily admit they never use the bells and whistles they pay a premium for when buying new products.

"At the time of purchase, people tend to focus on the positive and begin to imagine all the great uses they will get from these new features" says Wharton professor Robert J. Meyer. "But they fail to foresee all the things that will cause them not to use them, such as the difficulty of learning." In other words, just adding bells and whistles because you can doesn't always make sense, nor should it. We need to accept the fact that, sometimes, less is more.

VODAFONE: SIMPLE IS BETTER

Consumers are desperate for products that are simpler and less complex. Vodafone's latest cell phone model, called the Vodafone Simply, is aimed at the boomer crowd who want to make and receive phone calls without the added hassles of browsers and cameras and videos. Aimed at keeping "feature creep" in check, the phone is designed to simply make and receive calls and text messages, period.

According to a report from the BBC, the desire for a simplified handset, especially among the older crowd, was borne out by a Cap Gemini study conducted last year in Britain, which indicated that 80 percent of people over fifty-five preferred the basic approach. Vodafone is one of the few carriers that are listening, but watch for more and more "simplexity" (i.e., complex technology encased in devices made simpler and more intuitive) items to creep into the marketplace.

MAINBOCHER: THE NO DRESS DRESS

In current fashion circles, "more" often seems to indicate "better," as well as to justify a higher price tag. It seems that the more stuff, froufrou, details, and embellishment you can put on a garment, the better. It's all about ostentatious, in-your-face, over-the-top finery that screams, "I'm designer, I'm expensive."

Thankfully, throughout the annals of fashion, there have always been a few lone rebels who have a different vision. While some designers are known for their flamboyance, others have been given accolades for their understated elegance. There have been many stylish women who inherently have known the value of this formula: Jacqueline Kennedy Onassis, Wallis Simpson, and Audrey Hepburn to name a few. Each woman epitomized simple elegance and understated good taste. Working in the first half of the twentieth century, designers such as Madame Vionnet, Coco Chanel, and Mainbocher all built successful couture houses on the concept of "less is more," even with a high price ticket.

Mainbocher in particular embraced the "less is more" concept. He was an American from Chicago whose real name was Main Rousseau Bocher. He rose from the obscurity of the Midwest to the heights of Paris couture and is best known for designing the "wedding dress of the century" for Wallis Simpson for her 1937 marriage to the Duke of Windsor. Mainbocher's designs were priced at the very highest end of the couture spectrum, yet they were all about invisible details and workmanship that didn't show. So much so that his look became known as the No Dress Dress. A Mainbocher label meant *invisible elegance.* From the start, his theme was understatement. His design formula epitomized the power of *pianissimo,* a musical term that on a score refers to the power of subtlety.

Only ladies of the Social Register could afford Mainbocher's prices. His simple sheaths and suits were impeccably tailored and perfect for any occasion, from lunch at the country club to shopping on Fifth Avenue to your husband's boss's cocktail party. Ladies were known to bring in their dresses for a new lining (this was called a tune-up) just like another status symbol of the Social Register, the Rolls Royce, to which Mainbocher's designs were constantly compared. There are also stories about designer wardrobes being left to children in a will, and siblings fighting one another over who got the Mainbocher dress. Forget about the silver and jewels.

During the 1930s, Mainbocher was the destination for women of class who wanted to be deemed dressed appropriately at all times. His models wore spotless white gloves, strings of pearls, hairbands with flat bows, simple shoes, and other discreet accessories that perfectly complemented his simple suits or stylish evening gowns.

Even though he started his couture house in 1929 during the Depression, his business flourished. His simple yet supremely tailored style projected elegance and confidence—just the ticket for uncertain times.

Mainbocher may have been one of the original Zen designers. He once said, "I have never known a really chic woman whose appearance was not, in large part, an outward reflection of her inner self. To be well turned out, a woman should turn her thoughts in."

The No Dress Dress, it turns out, wasn't really about fashion.

It was a statement that was supposed to reflect a woman's inner beauty. Now there's a wardrobe worth a million bucks.

Mainbocher never became the household name that his co-conspirator Coco Chanel did, but between them they eliminated froufrou in favor of quality and simplicity of design—and that is what people are *still* willing to pay for.

MINUTECLINICS: QUICK, I'M SICK!

Imagine a health care clinic run like a fast food joint. Sound sick? It's anything but. MinuteClinics is a healthy new health care strategy based on the premise that certain basic health problems can be more quickly and cheaply diagnosed and treated in a quick walk-in clinic than in a doctor's office or emergency room. The concept was developed by Steve Pontius after he and his five-year-old son waited three hours in an urgent care clinic for a three-minute diagnosis.

MinuteClinics are staffed by nurse practitioners instead of doctors. Most patients are typically seen within fifteen minutes. The clinics offer a menu approach similar to that of a fast food restaurant. They don't do complicated; the "fare" is limited, they're really good at the few things that they do, and they're quick and cheap. They are located in convenient places where the customer has to be anyway, such as inside Cub Foods grocery stores or your neighborhood CVS store.

MinuteClinics aren't meant to replace your relationship with your primary health care provider. Instead, they serve as a quick and convenient fix when you're laid low by one of many common ailments such as strep throat, a bladder infection, or a sinus infection. Research shows that more than 80 percent of all health care events in a family's life consist of fourteen very common ailments, most of which are treatable by a nurse practitioner.

The nurse practitioners are allowed to treat only certain illnesses or conditions; there is always a doctor on call, and provisions are made for emergency situations. The average fee for an immediate treatment is approximately $45.

MinuteClinics is growing fast. Backed with $15 million via Bain Capital Ventures and others, it is planning to grow to 350 clinics in twenty metropolitan areas by 2009. It's a catchy idea. Similar concepts are spreading like viruses and include FastCare, Medi Minute, and Solistera.

DAY OF NOTHING: Nothing to Sneeze At

In the summer of 2005, Sense Worldwide featured a snippet of information that I found fascinating. They reported on a new television programming strategy that featured absolutely nothing. Fine Living Network, a small 23 million–subscriber cable network in the United States, recently aired an eight-hour show called "Day of Nothing." The show, which was basically a series of beautiful nature scenes, had no actors, no writing, no music, and no commercials (now you've got *my* attention!). "Nothing" was offered to its viewers in the spirit of a gift as a way to launch a new fall season by actually showing the season.

Entertainment Weekly was so enamored of the idea that it put the program on its notable programs to watch list, "presumably because TV is better once you get rid of writers and actors."

MORE SIMPLICITY

Linda Tischler, a senior writer at *Fast Company,* wrote a feature on what I call design creep, or feature creep. She commented that the idea of less is more may indeed be "innovation's biggest paradox" when it comes to integrating technology into our everyday lives. "We demand more and more from the stuff in our lives— more features, more function, more power—and yet we also increasingly demand that it be easy to use. And in an Escher-like twist, the technology that's simplest to use is also often the most difficult to create."

Creating high-tech products that are easy to use *and* loaded with cool features may seem like a tall order, but businesses that simplify their processes and their products will find enormous payback. It's one of the best ways I know to make friends with the consumer.

LESS PERFECTION: WABI SABI

The Japanese have long understood the beauty of imperfection and the elegance of understatement. Many of their traditions embody a "less is more" approach where less is typically all that's required. This artful philosophy is at the heart of a practice known as wabi sabi.

In the book *Wabi-Sabi for Artists, Designers, Poets & Philosophers* by Leonard Koren, wabi sabi is described as "the beauty of things imperfect, impermanent, and incomplete." Wabi sabi is a difficult idea for many to comprehend, let alone appreciate. In many ways it's the antithesis of the "more, bigger, and perfect" lifestyle that Americans tend to value.

Perhaps the best way to illustrate the concept behind wabi sabi is through a story, or allegory, that has been handed down through the centuries. It goes like this: Back in the 1500s, a tea master named Rikyu was asked to rake the leaves of his superior's courtyard. He was meticulous in completing his task, taking time to rake up every leaf, twig, and petal that had fallen to the ground. When he was finished, he put away his rake, then went back and surveyed the courtyard. After a moment or so he walked over to the cherry tree in the corner and shook it ever so gently until just a few blossoms scattered to the ground. Only then was his task complete. In Rikyu's eyes, an imperfect yard is the perfect yard.

For the new rebuilt M. H. de Young Memorial Museum in San Francisco, artist Andy Goldsworthy was commissioned to create a stone sculpture court at the museum's entrance. Goldsworthy chose to incorporate a wonderfully elegant wabi sabi element within his design: A delicately chiseled hairline fracture runs from the curb to the front door and passes through every stone and boulder in its path. The fracture serves as an homage to the earlier De Young museum, which was badly damaged in the 1989 earthquake, and offers a reminder to all of us about the temporal nature of our world. Wabi sabi, indeed.

A more "domestic" wabi-sabi story was given to me by a designer whose grandchild had wiped his paint-covered fingers on the side of her newly upholstered sofa while her back was momentarily turned. Instead of reprimanding the child, she chose to celebrate the wabi-sabi moment. She took the child by his paint-stained hands back over to the sofa and helped him paint his initials onto the "artwork." By choosing not to reupholster the sofa, she went the wabi-sabi way. In her eyes, the couch was now imperfectly perfect.

I don't know of too many grandparents who would react to that situation in the same manner. Thankfully, there are other ways to appreciate and celebrate the art of wabi sabi.

NATURE: IMPERFECTLY PERFECT

Wabi sabi is the mundane made exquisite. It's about taking an obscure everyday object and celebrating its natural state. Georgia O'Keeffe was a master at taking a found object in nature and elevating it to a masterpiece. A simple flower, a cow's skull, a rock, all became objects worthy of contemplation and appreciation. In the world of wabi sabi, simple natural elements and materials are greatly valued. Mud, paper, wood, and bamboo are prized above gold, silver, and diamonds.

Wabi sabi also celebrates imperfection in nature—the very naturalness of the environment, if you will. A gardening craze has taken our country by storm. Cultivating a bit of nature in your own backyard is a quest that for many requires hours of meticulous care and planting, feeding, and grooming.

Volumes have been written to show us how to have a perfectly themed and designed garden. Suburban garden centers have multiplied across the country, and television shows on gardening have proliferated on every network. There are even networks entirely devoted to the subject. Supermarkets and home stores carry a surplus of garden-inspired home-decorating items. City dwellers opt for window boxes and container gardeners turn their rooftops into landscaped wonders.

In the midst of this quest to tame nature, there's a new (or very old) approach to gardening that's growing in popularity. The idea is to have a landscape artfully designed to look undesigned. In true Zen style, nature is allowed to follow its own course. Items are carefully placed to look as if they've always been there. Grasses, ferns, and moss take center stage over blossoms, shrubs, and shoots. A lot of work goes into a wabi-sabi garden to make it look as if it "just happened."

ART OF IMPERFECTION: MUSSED, TATTERED, AND CRACKED

Wabi sabi is the mussed made stylish. Actress Meg Ryan was one of the first to make the wabi-sabi haircut an in-demand hairstyle at salons across the country. Her $300 haircuts, styled by Sally Hershberger, stylist to the stars, were intentionally chopped, tousled, and mussed to look, well, naturally imperfect.

Today you can buy styling products that will help you get that look. Bedhead is a best-selling line of hair styling products that will help you have hair like Meg Ryan's. The idea is that you get up in the morning and wash, dry, and style your hair. When you're done, you use the product to mess your hair up to look as though you just got out of bed.

Wabi sabi celebrates the worn, the tattered, and the torn. The *New York Times* featured a story in their Home Style section titled "Crumbled to Perfection." The article pointed out that newsstands today are packed with magazines selling the simple country life, and that while Prada-clad fashionistas may shudder, country style is back on the radar. For example, magazines such as *Country Living* and *Country Home* are among the best-selling shelter magazines on the market these days.

The article also says, "Some people are content to visit ruins, but some prefer to live in them full time!" Shabby Chic and Anthropologie have both taken that concept to a new retail level with their low-key home product lines that promote the worn, imperfect look. Items such as old-fashioned quilts, hand-embroidered pillows, and tableware and lamps that feature the faux patina of time are all in big demand.

Real life is messy. Things chip and break and crack. Carefully designed objects turn out irregular despite our best efforts at perfection. Tables get nicked, dinged, and spotted with watermarks. Porcelain cracks and pottery glazes drip and turn out inconsistent. To some, this is a disaster. To others, it's a subtle reminder that only the divine is perfect.

Metropolitan Home featured an article in their Trend Watch section in the summer of 2005 called "Wise Cracks." They reported that "artists and designers are going for broken—adding intentional fractures, fissures, and flaws to make pieces that are perfectly imperfect."

In the magazine, pieces of sculpture, pottery, and furniture, from contemporary designers such as Jason Miller, Anthony Brozna, and Dror Benshetrit, were showcased as the "shattering" new look in home design products. Prices ranged from $35 to $6,000. Obviously, imperfection doesn't come cheap.

LOW KEY, HIGH CLASS

The wabi-sabi "holiday" may be the chic-est of all. The title of a recent travel piece in *British Elle Décor* was "Are You Having a Shack Attack?" The premise is an expensive getaway vacation that allows you to experience firsthand what it is like to live the primitive, rustic life. It's perfect for those who have overdosed on Cristal, perma-tans, and diamond-encrusted everything. Your wilderness may be rustic and miles away from civilization, but the coffee is probably Starbucks, the futon is undoubtedly down, and you are chauffeured to your wilderness environment via a chartered luxury helicopter.

Forget five-star resorts. A wabi-sabi vacation is a cabin on a deserted island, a hut on a remote beach, a hammock gently swinging between two palms, a teepee in the mountains. The new vacation chic has little to do with jet-set luxury and everything to do with low-key yet extravagant hideaways.

THE ART OF ZEN: SIMPLY STYLISH

Wabi sabi at its best can be correlated to Zen Buddhism, which emphasizes the importance of transcending, or thinking beyond what is expected. It has been called "the beauty of poverty," referring to the delicate balance between the pleasures we get out of things and the pleasure we get out of the freedom from things.

Bringing wabi sabi into your life doesn't require money, training, or special skills. It takes a mind quiet enough to appreciate muted beauty, the courage not to fear bareness, and a willingness to accept things as they are. What's really required is a Zen approach to "letting go" to understand this simple but elusive philosophy.

CONCLUSION

Our basic human tendencies are hard to overcome. Some of us will never believe that less can be more, that imperfect will sell, or that bigger isn't better. But others are eager to embrace the state of grace arrived at through wabi sabi. Leonard Koren sums it up beautifully: "Pare down to the essence, but don't remove the poetry." That's keeping it simple . . . with style.

CHAPTER 6
HEALTHY INDULGENCES

OUR 24/7, ALWAYS-ON-THE-GO LIFESTYLES ARE TAKING A toll on our health. Despite the alleged promise of technology—of less work and more play—most of us are working harder than ever. We never really seem to get to the end of our must-do list so we can shift over to our want-to-do list. We are challenged to find enough leisure time to regularly exercise outdoors or at the gym. Instead, we often cope with our stress by looking for small indulgences and little pleasures that make our hectic lives seem more bearable.

It's certainly true in my life. After a long day at the office or on the road, I'm ready for a treat. I feel that I've more than earned a chocolate truffle, a relaxing massage, or a fabulous gourmet meal. Yet at the same time, I'm trying to take better care of myself, eat healthier, and exercise more. How to do both?

NUTRITIONAL SCHIZOPHRENIA:
All the Hubba Hubba, Half the Ding Ding

Wouldn't it be great if there were food sensations and experiences that tasted great and at the same time were actually good for you? Today, when foods or products fall short on satisfying taste buds, they fall short, period. Bottom line, we consumers want to have our cake, and we want to eat it too. We want, as a popular commercial says, "all the hubba hubba, and half the ding ding."

For many of us, diet is a four-letter word that means "deprivation." We are constantly looking for quick-fix, rapid ways to lose weight in an attempt to fend off the results of too many indulgences. The market for low carb, low calorie, low sugar, and low fat moved on to no carb, zero calories, Splenda-sweetened, and no fat. Zero became the new quest.

As a result, nutritional schizophrenia reigns. I have several friends who frequently order a salad for lunch with dressing on the side, pass on the bread, drink water with their meal, all so they can indulge in that gooey piece of chocolate cake.

Others' version of a diet consists of ordering a hamburger, fries, and *diet soda* at a fast food restaurant. I have my own odd little habit. I order a tall skim hot chocolate at Starbucks, but I still want the whipped cream. Doesn't seem to faze the baristas in the least.

At one time, many people imagined that the ultimate diet would be a medical miracle drug, a pill on a plate if you will. However, with the trend toward comfort and nesting, most consumers are no longer looking to science for a magic pill. They realize there would be very little satisfaction in living life that way.

More and more we're beginning to realize that it's really all about a healthy lifestyle and not about the latest diet craze or weight-loss fad. We embrace the idea that everything is acceptable, on occasion, in small doses. The new mantra is: Do more, eat less, but eat well.

THE FRENCH FOOD PARADOX

Lately, we're looking across the Atlantic to the French for the ultimate diet solution. Ironic, isn't it, that the French, purveyors of heavy sauces, foie gras, wine with every meal, and decadent desserts, just may have the solution to our nutritional schizophrenia?

A recent best-selling book, *French Women Don't Get Fat: The Secret of Eating for Pleasure* by Mireille Guiliana, does the near impossible—it's a diet book that doesn't involve dieting at all. Instead, Guiliana's advice is simple common sense: Eat in moderation, but eat three meals a day. Avoid processed foods. Don't snack. But at the same time, don't be afraid to have dessert. Oh . . . and walk everywhere.

Ms. Guiliana's approach has been called the French food paradox by some because she describes a way of eating and living that satisfies our taste buds but still manages to keep our waistlines in check. It achieves the ultimate food nirvana. We get to savor both our food and our *life*.

3 VODKA

Soy is known to contain cancer-fighting antioxidants, and many of us already opt for soymilk on our breakfast cereal. But now, it's possible to enjoy those same indisputable health benefits in your predinner martini.

3 Vodka is made from soy. *USA Today* said, "Given the miraculous properties attritubed to soy and to vodka, who's to say that combining the two won't be a match made in heaven?" What's so special about 3 Vodka? It's the first time in history that soy has ever been distilled. And, the proprietary, time-intensive

3 Vodka, made from soy

distillation method used makes it not only healthy but exceptionally smooth. As 3 Vodka's tagline states: "All things in life seek balance. 3 is what happens when vodka finds it."

3 Vodka comes in an eye-catching bottle with an enlarged red numeral 3, which is topped with a black plastic cap that doubles as a half-shot measuring device. Now that's what I call spirited trend blending, a healthy buzz, and a paradox in a bottle.

FUNCTIONAL CANDY: SWEET REVENGE

We're all familiar with what is now called functional food. That thought isn't so much paradoxical as it is redundant. Food is supposed to keep our bodies fueled. It's like the gas we put in our automobiles. We wouldn't get very far without it. And it doesn't matter whether we use unleaded, regular, or super premium. It pretty much gets us where we're going.

The idea of functional candy implies something different. Most candy is consumed for pleasure. But now there's a new twist to the candy offerings: candy that's really and truly good for you. Chews and lollipops are fortified with calcium; gummies and hard candy are enriched with vitamins and minerals. The number of low-glycemic-index sweets is growing, and sugar-free gum and mints have proven their popularity as market movers. Functional candy is a huge trend driven by our overall quest for a healthier lifestyle.

HEALTH BY CHOCOLATE

When I was a teenager dealing with the trauma of acne, I was told to lay off the french fries and the chocolate if I wanted my skin to clear up. Well, it didn't work. And for years I felt guilty whenever I indulged in a chocolate treat.

Times have changed. Now there's healthy chocolate. Is there really such a thing, you ask? The good news is yes! Health by Chocolate is a Swiss chocolate that's actually good for your skin. It's chock-full of antioxidants, minerals, omega 3 fatty acids, lutein, and lycopene, and it has as much fiber as an apple. It's also low glylcemic, so it releases its sugar slowly.

You can indulge your chocolate cravings in several ways. There's a dark chocolate candy bar, a Health by Chocolate Organic Instant Bliss Beauty Drink, and a Health by Chocolate Organic Women's Wonder Bar. The Wonder Bar is made just for women. It promises sweet revenge on PMS, menopause, and everyday cravings. The Swiss chocolate bar contains rose oil, herbs, and soy and was designed to help restore a woman's frame of mind while satisfying her chocolate cravings. Sounds like a medical miracle to me.

The products are made by Ecco Bella, a manufacturer and marketer of organic and natural products based in Wayne, New Jersey. Ecco Bella's mission is to offer products with the finest ingredients that are designed to provide consumers with high-quality alternatives to foods that they crave but generally try to stay away from for health reasons. In other words, they want to deliver on the hubba hubba, and they've taken out most of the ding ding.

Health by Chocolate is a decadent treat that promises to give you soft, smooth, luxurious-looking skin in a healthy yet indulgent manner. The paradox: Now you can be bad and still look good!

THE SPORT BEAN: PORTABLE POWER

Jelly Belly took a leap of faith and developed the first jelly bean designed for sports performance. Taking a cue from marathon runners who use jelly beans for a quick energy boost, the company decided to throw their hat into the $3.2 billion sports drink/food industry.

Sport Beans come in lemon lime and orange flavors, and are larger than the beans we usually associate with Jelly Bellys. These traditional-size jelly beans contain something extra. Each 1-ounce serving contains 25 grams of carbohydrates, 20 percent of the daily value for vitamins C and E, and 120 milligrams of electrolytes to boost energy and prevent dehydration. They're positioned to appeal to competitive athletes, sports enthusiasts, and anyone looking for a fast, refreshing energy source.

The functional jelly bean is packaged in 1-ounce bags, each the equivalent of 100 calories. It seems that not only do customers want more health benefits in their candy, they also want power to control their overall intake. Smaller, individual packaging takes the pain out of counting calories and reduces temptation.

Sport Beans have found a market with cyclists and long-distance runners. Kirk Albers, team captain of the Jelly Belly/ PoolGel pro cycling team, says, "Sport Beans taste better than the sports gels—and there are no sticky handlebars after eating them." I guess you could say they're clean good fun!

WHOLE FOODS: A WHOLE NEW BALL GAME

Not that long ago, natural food co-ops and organic health food stores were thought of as places where old hippies went to shop for their granola, soy milk, and tofu. They were cramped, ill lit, and located in out-of-the-way places. Everyone thought health food was a niche market that would never amount to anything. Well, it's a whole new ball game these days.

In fact, America is fast becoming a Whole Food nation. The all-natural organic supermarket chain is the fastest-growing grocery chain in our country, with 181 stones throughout North America and the United Kingdom. Today, Whole Foods is the world's largest retailer of natural and organic foods.

Fortune magazine called Whole Foods "the company that disdains hormones [and] had financials that look as if they're on steroids." They report that margins are almost twice that of most traditional grocery chains. That's because organic foods can carry a price premium of 40 to 175 percent over regular foods. Whole Foods pulls down around $800 per square foot in sales, which is double the industry average. Since going public in 1992, its stock is up nearly twenty-five fold.

Shopping at Whole Foods is an experience. *USA Today* calls it "shopping as showtime" and "the grocery equivalent of

DisneyWorld for food junkies." They go on to report that the all-natural grocery chain is "beloved by soccer moms and Hollywood starlets, as well as the organically inclined." In other words, it is now mainstream. So much so that many consumers call it Whole Paycheck.

Why are shoppers willing to pay more than they otherwise would at their local Safeway or Cub stores? Today, consumers are demanding higher food quality, especially when it comes to fresh produce and natural perishables. They recognize that healthy indulgence comes at a premium. In addition to the extensive sampling, theatrical staging, and exotic presentation, Whole Foods offers something beyond the usual earthy health food assortment. You'll find everything from artisan cheeses, organic Turkish apricots, and fine wines to top-of-the-line organic meats, free-range chicken, and an assortment of seafood as broad as Seattle's famous Pike Place Market.

But customers will also find fresh hot doughnuts (with no artificial ingredients), baked Alaska in the pastry section, and even Natural Cheetos. Yes, that's right. American college kids' favorite snack food is now offered in an all-natural organic version. Call them an oxymoron in a bag or an enchanting paradox. These new natural Cheetos-brand puffed snacks are made with natural white cheddar cheese and have no preservatives, no hydrogenated oils, and nothing artificial. As co-president Walter Robb comments, "We're not Holy Foods. We're Whole Foods." Amen.

YALE SUSTAINABLE FOOD PROJECT: ORGANICS 101

When I went to college, the school cafeteria was a haven where we were fed three hot meals a day. It wasn't exactly gourmet fare, but it was hot, and I didn't have to cook it. Nor did it encourage the healthiest of eating habits. I remember a lot of mashed potatoes (counterfeit authentic, of course), fried meats, and pizza. I also remember taking dozens of butter pats back to my dorm room for buttered popcorn, my nightly indulgence for study marathons. At this point, I should also mention that I did, in fact, gain the typical "freshman twenty" pounds my first year of college.

So, I was amazed when I learned about the Yale Sustainable Food Project. It's a joint endeavor of Yale University Dining Services, students, faculty, and administrators. According to their Web site, yale.edu/sustainablefood, "It's designed to nourish a culture in which the interwoven pleasures of growing, cooking, and sharing food become an integral part of each student's experience at Yale."

Though it may sound elitist and far-fetched, it's not. The program is a huge success, and the idea has turned into a movement. Since its inception, there's been a rash of fake ID cards made by nonstudents who try to sneak into the dining halls wearing school-insignia sweatshirts that help them look as if they belong. Seems some will do just about anything to have at the burgers of "grass fed lamb and fresh picked mint . . . chicken brodo with pasta and greens . . . and pork loin with fennel," according to an article in the *New York Times.* Some students are even thinking about starting a petition to take the concept campus-wide to Yale's 4,800-plus students.

The idea came about when Alice Waters's (owner of Berkeley's Chez Panisse restaurant) daughter became a freshman at Yale. Waters, long known for her celebration of local and seasonal ingredients and advocacy of natural and organic ingredients, wanted to bring the same healthy concept to her daughter's dining hall at college.

The program is based on the same tenets that make Chez Panisse such a perennial success—menus comprised of locally grown seasonal produce, much of it organic and all of it picked and served fresh. The farmers who grow the food practice the high standards of organic and natural farming, as do the ranchers who care for and feed their livestock using humane and ecological methods.

Yale students are actively involved all along the way, so the program is educational as well as nutritional. Initially, they helped clear land for an organic garden and created a compost program. All told, they planted 170 varieties of vegetables, fruits, flowers, and herbs, all of which are used in the meals as well as sold at the New Haven farmers' market.

Special guest speakers are a part of the educational program. Professors develop special academic curricula, such as The Psychology, Biology, and Politics of Food as taught by Professor Kelly Brownwell. The program occasionally sponsors events and symposiums, such as a recent day-long conference called Tilling the Soil, Turning the Tables that engaged students, dining service directors, and farmers from around the region in a discussion about bringing local, sustainable food to other college dining halls.

College dorm food that's really good for you? That just may be the ultimate food paradox.

HEALING RETREATS: JUST WHAT THE DOCTOR ORDERED

Not that long ago, when you considered a spa experience, you thought about relaxing massages, luxurious pedicures, and steamy facials, not necessarily about getting healthy. A hot-oil treatment or mud wrap was a special and exotic treat. And you probably didn't go that often. After all, it was a guilty pleasure that many viewed as self-indulgent.

Today, with our fast-paced world and time-starved lives, visiting a spa has become an earned reward for surviving the daily grind. The spa industry is responding by offering a new kind of experience that is more health minded. However, in no way are they sacrificing anything on the luxury end of the equation.

I experienced this concept firsthand when I took a healing retreat vacation at Chiva-Som in Hua Hin, Thailand. Chiva-Som is Thai for "Haven of Life." It is essentially a private luxury health resort. While there, I received analyses and coaching from a vast team of doctors, nurses, dieticians, and qualified natural health practioners. I also experienced Reiki, a life-coaching session with a Buddhist monk, daily massages, meditation sessions, yoga, and chi gong sessions, as well as three healthy spa-cuisine meals a day.

I learned about the differences between the Western and Eastern approaches to health. Essentially, Western medicine is about treating illness by addressing the symptoms, while Eastern medicine is more of a wellness approach, focused on preventing the symptoms in the first place. It was an eye-opening experience, and I came home relaxed, rejuvenated, and armed with knowledge and tools to help me live a healthier life.

According to a Trends & Predictions Study conducted by *Spa Finder* magazine, this new phenomenon (they dub it "the medical spa") is one of the hottest trends in the spa industry. These spas are staffed by medical doctors, not just aestheticians and fitness consultants, and they take an integrative and holistic approach to health. And these are anything but sterile medical facilities. These medical spas offer soothing environments that are especially conducive to healing. They specialize in integrating the mind, body, and spirit into the healing aspects of the spa experience.

Baby boomers, in particular, are embracing the healing aspects of medical spas. They are accustomed to wanting to make the most of their lives, and this format provides a healthy alternative to today's more rigid medical system.

My experience was life changing. Chiva-Som for me was a healthy indulgence in the best sense of the word. I left with a healthier body, yes. But I also gained a lasting sense of inner peace, contentment, and fulfillment that I'd never have found at a conventional spa.

CONCLUSION

We all want to live better lives, and our approach to meeting that goal is becoming less reactive and more proactive. While we used to go to the doctor because we were ill, today we go in order to stay well. The paradox lies in the fact that rather than a dreaded treatment, it's become a healthy indulgence to visit the doctor and to have our overall wellness issues addressed in a holistic fashion.

CHAPTER 7
COUNTERFEIT AUTHENTICITY

THERE IS A HEIGHTENED DEMAND IN THE WORLD TODAY FOR products that are authentic, that have a heritage that they are true to, and that stand for something that is real and inherently good. In the food world, for example, artisan breads, estate-grown olive oils, heirloom tomatoes, and special vintage wines are now requested by name. It matters, very much, that they are real and that their provenance is authentic.

Recipes these days don't call for apples, but for red Pippin or Jupiter apples. Syrups aren't just syrup, they're Vermont maple or wild Maine blueberry. There's even a special orange juice from blood oranges from the island of Sicily that are identified by the fact that they are grown not merely in Sicily, or even Italy, but in the volcanic soil of Mount Etna. Along the same lines, ethnic is no longer just Italian or French or Asian. Instead, it's Tuscan or Umbrian, Provencal or Basque, or Thai or Vietnamese.

The craving for authenticity is often at the heart of what drives our brand purchases. When a shoe or T-shirt comes with the Nike swoosh, you know you're getting the real thing. When your shampoo is rosemary mint from Aveda, you can be certain that the ingredients are natural and authentic. When your polo shirt has the embroidered Polo player or the LaCoste alligator appliqué, you are telling the world that the real thing matters very much to you. Even Coke tries to connect with consumers and capitalize on the fact that they are The Real Thing when it comes to cola.

Interestingly, however, there is a major backlash—or countertrend—to all of this authenticity. I call it counterfeit authenticity—products, services, and experiences that are in-your-face fake, and proud of it. They deliberately mimic the real thing to the degree that some people actually prefer the fake or counterfeit item over the real thing.

It seems that somewhere along the line, our perfectionist natures have compulsively driven us to take what many think is already perfect (Mother nature, national shrines, even the air we breathe) and make it better by making it fake.

The other day I was enjoying a motorcycle ride through the countryside of Wisconsin when my antennae picked up on an interesting rural outdoor décor trend. Along the back roads of Lake Winnebago, many homeowners had strategically placed obviously fake plastic deer on their lawns. Some featured an antlered buck crossing into the woods, followed tentatively by a smaller doe and a spotted fawn or two. Others displayed fawns curled up sleeping at the feet of their parents, who were pausing on their trek across the yard to let junior sleep.

As we cruised along, the late afternoon shadows began to

shift, and I noticed something a little different on one homeowner's lawn. It was a doe rendered so perfectly that you could actually see the hairs on her body. Her eyes glistened dark and alert. I even thought I saw her nose whiskers twitch. I remember thinking, now that homeowner obviously has great taste. They must have gone out of their way to find such an authentic fake statue to display on their lawn.

Then, as you might guess, the noise of the bike cruising by caused the obviously *not* fake deer to scamper off into the woods. I realized I had just witnessed a good lesson in counterfeit authenticity. I had been duped into thinking that the real thing was a fake! Which got me to thinking, what is real? And what is fake? What makes something faux, and is that just a nice word for fake? And what constitutes authenticity anyway? Is it, like beauty, only realized in the eyes of the beholder?

Let's explore some of the unique products and experiences that demonstrate this trend. In each case there's a distinct advantage to selling the consumer something that's obviously fake. That's part of the magic of this paradox.

LAS VEGAS: Virtual Venice/Fiberglass France

I recently heard Las Vegas described as a "virtual Venice" and a "fiberglass France." When you think about it, the entire Las Vegas experience is a perfect example of what's being called the theme parking of America. The gambling mecca is a single destination, where visitors can feign the experience of the other *real* world without leaving the city limits. Take a walk down the strip and you can sample New York City, complete with the Statue of Liberty. You can see the pyramids of Egypt, the Eiffel Tower of Paris, stroll and shop the canals of Venice, or watch a pirate battle at Treasure Island.

For many, the carefully controlled environment beats the real thing. The scale is more human, feels safer, and is in many cases cleaner—and probably a whole lot cheaper—than the real thing. Best of all perhaps, these champions of Vegas are never more than a minute away from a chance to win big at the gaming tables. For them, that's a big win.

MISSION TO MARS:
Stratospheric Counterfeit Authenticy

Maybe you'd rather go to Mars. Leave it to Disney, the ultimate purveyors of virtual reality, to take the counterfeit authentic concept over the top and into outer space.

Mission to Mars, a special attraction sponsored a few years ago by Hewlitt-Packard, actually sought to transport consumers to another planet. The attraction was designed with the full support of NASA and was reported to have cost Disney more than $100 million to develop and construct. Purported to be their most technologically advanced attraction when it opened, it relied on visual imaging, motion control, and centrifuge technology to send would-be astronauts on a futuristic voyage to the red planet.

Disney literally launched riders into a pulse-racing liftoff complete with the sensations of traveling through outer space.

Unlike a carnival ride (remember the Gravitron?) where you're simply strapped in and whirled around for a few moments in the open air, riders were ensconced inside what amounts to a full-flight simulator. The capsule featured individual monitors, control sticks to move, and buttons to push.

Add to that layers of audio, video, lighting, and special effects and you've got an incredibly immersive experience. According to a Disney press release, "When the countdown reaches zero, the most unique and exhilarating ride experience ever begins. The earth begins to rumble, white clouds of exhaust start to stir as the ascent toward the sky starts, and guests are rocketed into the galaxies."

When Disney launched this program in 1993, they were pioneering virtual interactive reality to a degree unheard of before in the entertainment venue. Guests assumed the role of commander, pilot, navigator, or engineer and were actually asked to perform vital tasks that would land their spacecraft safely on Mars. Ultimately, the riders took a virtual trip into a faux reality. In an article on the NASA Web site at the time, Michelle Viotti, from the Jet Propulsion Laboratory, was quoted as saying, "This ride brings it home and makes it real." That's a great testimonial to the ultimate counterfeit authentic experience.

RAINFOREST CAFÉ: Your Safari Is Waiting

If landing on Mars is a little too "out there" for you, you can do something more earthbound but still a bit on the wild side and enjoy a great meal at the same time. Simply take a trip to a Rainforest Café, a restaurant escape where you can experience tropical rainstorms while animatronic elephants, butterflies, and monkeys come to life table side, parrots shriek from their perches in the exotic flora and fauna, and tanks of brilliant fish swim between sections.

Your safari guides (waiters and waitresses) will help you navigate the exotic menu, through fresh and unusual juices and smoothies, pasta, pizza, steak, salads, stir fry, and more. Everything they do at the Rainforest Café is intended to deliver a counterfeit authentic experience. For instance, when your table is ready, they announce it by saying, "Anderson party, your adventure is about to begin." And if you miss your call, the announcement is, "Anderson party, the safari is leaving without you."

End your dining adventure with a Rainforest coffee concoction and a tropical-theme dessert: Key lime or tortoise ice cream pie, "gorillas in the mist banana cheesecake," or perhaps their special sparkling volcano dessert, guaranteed to knock your socks off. As you leave the café, you can't miss the rain-forest-and animal-theme gift shop. It's a real link to civilization, the last leg of your journey back to the real jungle out there—the mall.

MAYDAYCARD SERVICE:
Postcards Without the Hassle of Travel

We're all familiar with that sharp pang of envy we feel when someone we know jets off to yet another exotic location on the other side of the world. Well now, if you're absolutely desperate to "keep up with the Joneses" without putting yourself into debt or hopping onto a plane, a solution is at hand. A company that sends actual handwritten postcards from far-flung destinations—on behalf of people who have never even been there—is reportedly doing excellent business. MayDayCard company, the "alibi post office," sends your greetings from a journey you never even took. They collect personally written cards (in your authentic handwriting) and send them for you from a variety of expensive holiday destinations.

The German firm has found success by engaging in a novel form of counterfeit authenticity. Ironically, the scheme was created by a woman who said she herself never liked writing postcards. A team of twenty people, consisting of pilots, flight attendants, and the founder and her husband, collects people's personally written cards and posts them.

As their Web site, MayDayCards.com, says, you're only one mouse click away. "Take your choice. . . . Hawaii, Heidelberg, or another beautiful destination. Order the postcard with the corresponding stamp, write the card at home, and address it to whomever you want to impress." The company guarantees it will forward your card, by plane, to the local post office of your chosen destination in order to get the "official and genuine postmark."

Postcards without the hassle of travel. The ultimate counterfeit authentic travel experience is only a mouse click away.

HOME, FAKE HOME: Faux Châteaus

Americans love to think that their home is their castle. More and more, though, home sweet home is turning into home fake home. Many real materials are being replaced by faux versions that are, indeed, better than the real thing.

DAVINCI SLATE: FAKE SLATE

DaVinci Slate is marketed as a "renaissance in roofing" and promises "the look of slate without the weight." These innovative manmade shingles are a synthesis of state-of-the-art polymer chemistry, the latest injection-molding technology and a unique coloration process. The result, as their Web site says, is "the most authentic-looking synthetic slate shingles the world has ever seen . . . a true revolution in the art and science of roofing."

DaVinci's new material allows them to fabricate thick-yet-lightweight, easy-to-install shingles that have all the beauty, color-fastness, fire resistance, and timeless performance of the traditional residential roofing gold standard—the real thing, slate. The shingles are modeled from actual slate to ensure a classically coarse surface and naturally rough edges. They come pre-collated in bundles with five widths and a choice of nine "blends," comprised of distinctive combinations of nineteen different colors. You can also order your own custom blend for an extra fee (mass customization anyone?).

The suggested retail price is $415 to $515 per 100 square feet of coverage, a significant cost savings over the real thing. There are several other advantages to going with the fake slate as well. Quarried slate is very expensive, quite heavy, and difficult to work with. DaVinci's faux slate is easier to lift and to ship, and it offers some functional advantages as well. The Lenexa, Kansas-based company said the shingles can be cut with a utility knife and that they remain pliable at 40 degrees below zero, don't absorb water, and are certified to be Class A fire resistant.

Why put an ordinary roof on an extraordinary home? Every roof provides shelter, but only the most distinctive roofs can provide something more. DaVinci roofs promise beauty, character, and the grace to complement, but never eclipse, fine architecture. That sounds like a lot to promise for a "fake and proud of it" product, but DaVinci delivers big time. Their faux slate product has been so successful that they're now offering a new wood shake shingle lookalike—a fake shake in other words.

BACCHUS CAVES

Homes are getting bigger and bigger, even as the American family is getting smaller. It's amazing the lengths, or I should say depths, to which some people will go to add space to their homes. Bacchus Caves is a unique business that was launched in 1997 by David Provost and a team of experienced underground professionals. They offer homeowners the excavation and addition of a subterranean room to their homes, i.e., a fake cave.

Why a cave? Many people think caves are seductive, others think that they're just plain cool. (Bruce Wayne certainly did.) Bacchus is building caves to be used as dining rooms, libraries,

Bacchus Caves in California

romantic retreats, driving ranges, and home theaters. According to *USA Today,* one creative soul even wants a "fake natural" hot spring in his cave.

It turns out that one advantage is a substantial cost savings. For construction on land in the California area, for example, Bacchus's fees start at $150 per square foot compared to $500 per square foot. And it's easier to get permits to build as caves are subject to fewer technical regulations than additions or remodels.

"Fake natural" caves aren't just updated versions of the Flintstones's cartoon cave homes. They're high-tech custom-designed rooms that just happen to be twenty-five feet below the earth's surface. They are a perfect example of the sort of counterfeit authenticity that just may push the U.S. housing market to uncharted . . . depths.

PLAY: A New Make-Believe

When we were kids, playtime was an escape from the real world. Our parents used to encourage us to use our imaginations to invent games and stage make-believe tea parties or to wage war. I remember playing capture the flag, which was basically a game that simulated a war in which, by capturing the other team's flag, which was hidden in their territory, we won and ruled the world.

Today, kids use their imaginations in very different ways. Most spend their day in front of a screen of some sort, "observing" the real world from afar. Now, however, modern technology allows them to escape to a place that is as real as the real thing.

SSD'S XAVIXPORT: SIMULATED SPORTS

Bass fishing with no hooks to bait. Golf with no mosquitoes. Bowling without the funny shoes. Today's video games utilize advanced technology that takes the participant deep into a virtual reality. These high-tech gadgets seek to create a fake authentic experience, but one that's better than the original that they pattern themselves after.

Now, video-game enthusiasts can give more than just their thumbs a workout. Couch potatoes, prepare to sweat. SSD's XaviXPORT lets homebodies get physical with simulated sports. All you need is a XaviXPORT, a TV, and the system type (read "game") that you like best. To play, participants swing wireless controllers shaped like standard sports equipment such as bats and rackets. Let the games begin.

Living-room athletes may choose from activities such as tennis and golf, as well as bass fishing and bowling. Some versions offer life-size screens where you put yourself into the picture, and then observe the counterfeit authentic results of your activity.

NINTENDOGS: NEW DOG, OLD TRICKS

You can even have your pick of the litter without ever having to worry about cleaning up any "accidents." Nintendogs, Nintendo's latest pet simulation game, features an adorable litter of virtual puppies that jump, bark, and play just like the real thing. Well almost, anyway. The good news is that there's no mess, no meals, no allergies, no chewed shoes, and no kennel expenses when you go out of town.

Players choose a puppy from the kennel, pick out a name, and then repeat it over a microphone until the virtual Fido responds. Owners can play Frisbee with Fluffy, toss a tennis ball for Shep, or take Rover for a walk in the park. If you're the competitive type, you can also sign your puppy up for obedience courses and competitions.

I just wonder how it feels to nuzzle a screen instead of a warm wet nose.

FANTASY CAMPS: WHERE THE RUBBER MEETS THE ROAD

BMW's M School is a two-day fantasy camp for adults where aspiring amateurs can indulge in their passion to drive fast and go for the checkered flag. Driving schools that offer customers the opportunity to have a counterfeit authentic racetrack driving experience are very popular with dealers such as Porsche, Audi, and Jeep.

It's an experience that doesn't come cheap. At M School, students race high-performance M3 coupes (333 hp) and M5 sedans (400 hp) on racetracks that seek to authenticate a real race experience. *Time* magazine reported that "the requirements include $3,650.00, proficiency with a stick shift and an iron stomach."

Camp Jeep events, sponsored by Chrysler, create a vacation-like experience that takes city drivers off road for a taste of the real thing, complete with spinouts, thrills and chills, and tough lessons. It's an on-road experience that simulates an off-road adventure, where real rubber meets a fake road.

MOVIES AND MUSIC:
What You See or Hear Isn't Always What You Get

Through state-of-the-art film and music technology, virtually anything is now possible (at least, virtually). Fantasy is morphing into reality, and reality is morphing into fantasy—and consumers are embracing the counterfeit authenticity of it all.

POLAR EXPRESS

There's a new twist on reality at the movies too. The 2004 holiday hit *Polar Express,* starring Tom Hanks, launched a technological revolution in Hollywood. The production was neither live action nor computer animation but something in between. The results attracted adults as well as children to the story.

Technology was leveraged in a unique way that the industry called "performance capture." Basically, actors were digitized, i.e., turned into faux animated images. Real actors were made to look as though they were drawings, or put another way, authentic people were made to look fake.

Computers were also used to create faux backgrounds that looked real. *USA Today* reported that the director, Robert Zemeckis, said the movie "looked like an oil painting come to life." The author and illustrator of the best-selling children's book that inspired the movie talked about the "paradoxical quality of the film being the beneficiary of absolutely cutting-edge technology while telling an earnest, old-fashioned story."

The paradox was an express ride to profits at the box office.

MUSIC: I HEAR A SYMPHONY (AT LEAST I THINK I DO)

Zenph Studios, located in Raleigh, North Carolina, has developed a technology that can take a music recording and convert it into a live concert played on real instruments. Huh, you say?

New Scientist magazine reports that Zenph extracts the sounds from scratchy old audio recordings and converts them into a high-resolution version of a program that is considered a standard way of coding music for computers. The "concert" can then be played on a Disklavier Pro piano, one of a handful of concert grands that can record and play back high-definition files.

Based on the file, the piano will replicate every note struck on the original recording from the original concert, right down to the velocity of the hammer and the position of the key when it was played. According to *New Scientist,* "The results are note perfect." Except that it's fake.

On a similar note, many people are paying good money to hear "fake original" music at a hot joint in Danbury, Connecticut, called the Premier. For several hours a night, an extremely accomplished group of musicians called the Fab Faux perform golden oldies exactly as they were recorded by the original artists. According to Tim Manners of Cool News, these "accomplished copycats" perform with "astonishing authenticity, using the very same gear—Hoffners, Gretsches, Rickenbackers and Voxes" as the original artists.

These guys work hard to give you a fabulous fake music experience. They practice for hours on end, making sure that every "guitar lick and drum roll; every three-part harmony; every bass line, every hand clap and finger snap" is exactly the way we know it from the real thing.

Tim reports that these guys are serious about their art. No funny wigs, weird costumes, or lame impersonations. "This is tribute band as performance art; not an imitation but a replication."

In other words, it's great entertainment, and it's faux real.

Across the pond there's a story of another case of genuine fakes—but this impersonation landed a talented artist in prison. In March 2006, the *New York Times* reported on John Mayatt, the guy who Scotland Yard believes "may have committed the greatest art fraud of the 20th century."

Once a struggling artist, Mayatt turned to crime in order to feed his kids. He was hired by a shady agent to produce numerous copies of famous works of art—Klees, Giacomettis, Chagalls—that his business partner passed off to unsuspecting art buyers as original works of art . . . selling them for hundred of thousands of dollars.

His partner made millions. Mayatt made very little, and eventually quit the scheme in disgust. They were both eventually arrested and served time after being nabbed by Scotland Yard. Sarah Lyall, the reporter for the *New York Times*, reports that one of Mayatt's first customers after he served his short sentence was the detective who had put him behind bars.

Today, Mayatt makes a good honest living painting genuine fakes—only he's learned his lesson. Now, when he completes a work of art (he still spills black coffee on the fakes to make them look authentically old and original), he signs his masterpiece "genuine fake" in indelible ink on the back of the canvas.

Who says crime doesn't pay? Michael Douglas has bought the rights to make this tall tale with a happy ending into a movie.

DREAM DINNERS: Heating In

As time demands on families continue to increase, mealtimes offer much-needed opportunities for family catch-up and connecting.

Studies show that moms especially cherish mealtimes and will make the effort to transform dinner into family bonding time. Surprisingly, oftentimes it's not carving out the table time that's the problem. After all, we all need to eat. It's the shopping, prepping, cleanup, and even the planning that we can't find the time for. Who has time to cook a homemade meal anymore?

Meal assembly is a hot new trend that moms call a lifesaver and financial experts call one of the fastest-growing food trends in the country. The idea is to help Mom prepare a counterfeit authentic "homemade" meal, without having to do all the work involved in cooking the real thing. But Mom still gets to cook.

Dream Dinners offers her the perfect solution. This fast-growing chain allows women to put healthy, homemade meals on the table for weeks at a time, while spending only *two* hours in the "kitchen." The concept is simple. The rewards are great. Customers go online to sign up for a two-hour cooking session at a commercial kitchen. They select either six or twelve entrées, each of which serves four to six people, and then they show up on the appointed day with a cooler to take home what they make.

When they arrive at the kitchen, they find the ingredients for each entrée already sliced, diced, or chopped, with everything chilled and ready to be measured. They then follow the step-by-step recipes, with professional chefs overseeing their efforts, and assemble each entrée, adjusting (customizing!) ingredients to taste. No real cooking or baking is done on the premises. The food is packed in freezer bags or disposable aluminum containers. At the end of two hours, customers have enough ready-to-cook entrées to feed a family for weeks. And at a cost of just around $200 (that averages to less than $3 a portion), it's a budget saver too. It's not home cooking, mind you, but it allows customers to replicate the home-cooked experience without all the effort and time.

Dream Dinners founded the concept. It was conceived by two women in Seattle who hosted a girls' night out in a rented catering kitchen where friends could socialize as they prepared a month's worth of meals to be frozen and cooked later. It was such a hit that the two women decided to turn it into a business.

As of March 2006, Dream Dinners now has more than 112 outlets nationally, with another sixty-four planned for the near future; and others have caught on to this trend. Let's Dish, Dinner Helpers, Dinner's Ready, Super Suppers, Dinner by Design, and more have popped up around the country.

Part of the success of the concept is that it's also a social event. Clients are encouraged to book time in their kitchens with friends and neighbors so they can catch up while cooking. Talk about multitasking! And the best part is, you never have to wash a dish or pan.

The twist here is that it really *is* home cooking, it's just not cooked at home. Mom still makes it, but she has a lot of help along the way. What these companies ultimately have to offer is guilt-free convenience, customization, and a return to something civilized—a sit-down homemade family meal.

HEAT AND EAT: MEALS WITH WHEELS

There are other versions of this concept as well, and they've gone way beyond the heat-and-eat world of Swanson's frozen

TV dinners. Supermarkets offer meal kits and all-in-one pack-aged solutions as a service to their customers and charge a pre-mium for it while they're at it. Take-out meals from full-service restaurants are on the rise, too. Starved for time, but not willing to trade down on quality and experience, consumers find that takeaway meals offer them time-saving benefits without having to forgo the ingredients of a home-cooked meal.

White Toque, an importer of European frozen meals, is opening several stores here in the United States that offer hun-dreds of versions of deep-chilled gourmet meals. Examples of their selections include seafood paella, Cajun pork chops, salmon tartare, and garlic mashed potatoes.

Another related idea is the appeal of having a real top-notch restaurant in your very own fridge, freezer, or pantry. Over the past few years, mainstream brand-restaurant chains such as Legal Sea-food and California Pizza Kitchen, have introduced premade meals into the grocer's aisles. Even upscale restaurants such as Charlie Trotter's are getting into the game, prepackaging not just their food but their secret sauces and flavorings. Many seek to re-create the entire restaurant experience.

The "heating in" phenomenon creates a faux homemade ex-perience for consumers and their families without breaking their backs slaving in the kitchen, or breaking their budgets. And it probably helps to keep alive some semblance of family unity, pro-viding more time to spend together at the table, and less time working in the kitchen. Even Martha Stewart would probably say, "It may be fake, but it's a good thing."

BOTTLED AIR: Breathe Easy

Most of us consider the air we breathe to be a limitless natural resource, but someday fresh air may be considered the ultimate luxury. What if we could bottle it?

MAUI AIR: PARADISE PRESERVED . . . IN A BOTTLE

Some enterprising companies are taking this idea to heart—they're bottling the outdoors and taking it indoors. A Hawaiian company called Pure Hawaiian Air markets "Heaven in a Bottle," essentially bottled Maui air that they say is "Paradise Preserved." They offer you a way to take the fragrance of the islands home to the mainland by capturing the fresh aromas and lush experience of a Hawaiian vacation. You can re-create a counterfeit authentic version of your vacation with just a misting! Jon P. Farmer, creator of Jail Blazer Jam, is the owner and bottler. He reports that business is brisk, with thousands of bottles sold at more than $6 a crack.

In a major endorsement of this concept, consumers are increasingly flocking indoors for a breath of fresh air. Forget bottled water, which just a decade ago seemed eccentric. Bottled air is the hot new product. These days, oxygen bars are popular in smoggy cities such as Los Angeles, Bangkok, and Tokyo. You can now belly up to the bar and get twenty minutes of pure oxygen for about $20. Also, more and more products are appearing on the market, designed to deliver a hit of pure oxygen to your system in a portable manner.

The idea isn't just marketing "woo woo" or psychological bunk either. Scientists note that just three hundred years ago the density of oxygen in the environment on earth was 30 percent. Today it is 19 to 20 percent. In addition, there's been an increase in carbon monoxide in the air. The combined result is a decrease in the carrying capacity of oxygen in the blood. Studies show that humans have not adapted well. We've not become more efficient at extracting oxygen from the air, nor have we developed larger lungs to take in more air by volume. The side effects of these changes range from lower tissue oxygen levels, lower energy production, lower cellular function, lower glandular function, and a slow accumulation of toxins resulting in toxemia. Are you choking yet? Sounds as though this is one counterfeit authentic that we really need.

O PUR: PORTABLE PERSONALIZED OXYGEN

O Pur, manufactured in Great Britain, is a personal source for a blast of pure oxygen that promises to help make you feel good. It's basically an inhaler attached to a canister that contains eight liters of pure oxygen at a minimum of 99.5 percent purity. It contains no expellants, additives, preserving agents, or aromas.

O Pur claims the oxygen won't make you lightheaded, but they also acknowledge it won't make you run faster either. Instead, it takes you to a middle ground. For athletes, it promotes good belly breathing. It's also supposed to be great for a hangover. The benefits may actually be more psychological than any-thing, but many people think it's worth the counterfeit authentic experience.

RETAIL: Bringing the Great Outdoors Inside

Bottled oxygen is just one way of bringing the great outdoors in-doors. Interior decorators also have been working the trend in a different way. More and more Americans are seeking to re-create the great outdoors indoors.

Sears Great Indoors is a specific retail format designed to de-liver the experience of nature to those of us who prefer to stay inside. Many homeowners and apartment dwellers want to sur-round themselves with the serenity of nature, even if it's really just silk flowers, decorative twigs, or a container garden. Sun-rooms and indoor garden rooms feature materials such as slate floors and glass roofs, and are decorated with faux authentic wicker furniture to allow as much of Mother Nature inside as possible. You *know* you're inside, but the idea is to make you *feel* as though you are enjoying Mother Nature—on your terms.

Even paint companies want you to experience or at least en-vision nature with their paint products. Their logic implies that if the great outdoors is your idea of heaven, then create a haven that embraces it. Make Mother Nature your muse. Their ads and pho-tos invite you to put yourself in that "magical place where time stands still, the air is pure, and all you can hear is the hushed sound of a gentle breeze in the trees."

Apparently you can expect even more from that can of paint. Benjamin Moore suggests that by using their Studio Finishes you can achieve "the hushed calm of your garden," and that "the power of expression is all yours." A competitor entices you with an invitation to allow your soul to unfurl and bring the outdoors in by using the restful and restorative colors of nature. Rejuvenate in a room with a view where the bed feels like "it's floating on air." That's a lot of magic in a paint can!

Another paint company featured ads that asked "Where does your inspiration come from?" They then supplied the answer on their paint chip cards. Their sample color chips are painted in such a way that various shades of blue are represented by a photo of the sky or the ocean, greens by leaves and grass, etc. Beautiful photography highlights nature in a most realistic and desirable way.

It's not nice to fool Mother Nature, but in this case, the trend is real.

I recently attended an annual Harley Davidson National H.O.G. rally (as an observer, not a participant) that exemplified the counterfeit authentic experience. Here were all these middle-aged couples making a weekend of dressing the part and simulating the life of a biker. They *are* bikers, of course. Just not what we historically think of as the rebels portrayed in the movie *Easy Rider.*

They represent a new breed of the now-real thing, known as RUBbies, to be exact, a trend term for "Rich Urban Bikers." Many are accountants, lawyers, and retired professionals who want to escape their version of the real world and live in a different one, even if it's just for a limited amount of time. They ride real Harleys, wear authentic leather, and have come a long way in living out their biker-weekend fantasies. Events such as the H.O.G. rally even feature tents where you can get a "temporary" tattoo—i.e., a fake version of the real thing that lasts about a week instead of a lifetime.

When you really begin to look at your world through new eyes, you will see examples of counterfeit authenticity everywhere. We work out on StairMasters and rowing machines that simulate an outdoor run or crewing on the river. We relax lakeside in Adirondack chairs that look authentic but are in fact made of fiberglass recycled from old plastic pop bottles. We use air fresheners and scented laundry detergents that replicate the experience of the great outdoors.

Even cosmetic companies are beginning to realize that there is a new concept of real beauty that is being embraced by women across the country. You may have noticed all the press surrounding the Dove campaign that celebrates "real beauty" by featuring an obviously older woman who embodies a new version of beauty. They are, in effect, highlighting the *real* real thing, slight wrinkles, gray hair, and all. The implication is that the real thing may in fact be better than the manufactured virtual reality that for so long has been thrust on us by marketers who show nineteen-year-olds selling antiwrinkle treatments.

CONCLUSION

Perhaps it is time to rethink what reality is, what it should or could be, and what people really want anyway. Then, if you can embrace the ideas of two opposing realities in your head at the same time, some unique possibilities may present themselves along the way.

CHAPTER 8
EXTREME RELAXATION

YOU'VE HEARD OF WORKING HARD AND PLAYING HARD. BUT have you ever thought about *relaxing hard*?

On average, Americans work 350 hours per year longer than our peers in Western Europe do. We're putting in longer hours on the job now than we did in the 1950s despite promises of a coming age of leisure in the new millennium. The year 2000 has come and is long gone and, bottom line, we're working more than medieval peasants did who, scholars estimate, worked between 120 and 150 days a year. Certainly life was harder back then, but we're also working more than the citizens of any other industrial country today. Add to that the fact that working Americans average a little more than two weeks of vacation per year, while Europeans average five to six weeks and you have a recipe for mass exhaustion.

The www.takebackyourtime.org Web site is dedicated to helping us live better lives by showing us other ways to live. Take Back

Your Time Day is a nationwide initiative to challenge the epidemic of overwork, overscheduling, and time famine that now threatens our health, our families and relationships, our communities, and our environment.

National Take Back Your Time Day is celebrated each year on October 24. The idea is that if we all stopped working on that day and didn't go back to work for the rest of the year, we, as working Americans, would have put in as many hours on the job as the rest of the civilized world does in a year's time.

France—a very civilized country—has long been associated with the thirty-five-hour week. In a clever piece in the *New York Times Magazine*, Charles McGrath notes that "there was time when the 35-hour workweek was the envy of the world, and especially of Americans, who used to travel to France just so they could watch the French relax."

The Take Back Your Time Foundation points out that overwork hurts us all in different ways. Overwork threatens our health. It leads to fatigue, accidents, and injuries. It reduces time for exercise and encourages consumption of calorie-laden fast foods. Experts estimate that job stress and burnout cost our economy more than $200 billion a year. It also threatens the fabric of our country. Overwork threatens our marriages, families, and relationships as we find less time for one another, less time to care for our children and elders, less time just to hang out and *relax*.

It weakens our communities. We have less time to know our neighbors, supervise our young people, and volunteer. It leaves us little time for ourselves, for self-development, or for spiritual growth. It even contributes to the destruction of our environment. Studies show that not having enough time encourages the use of convenience and throwaway items and reduces recycling.

Most of us can't even imagine having a thirty-five-hour workweek. The idea of twice-yearly vacations is an unrealized luxury to many. The notion of quitting work for the year on October 24 may sound silly, but it should provoke some serious thought about extreme relaxation.

American lives have gotten way out of balance. Given the mandatory long hours and the conspicuously absent vacations, how can we offset the negative effects of overwork? This chapter highlights more examples of the effects of overwork and showcases a variety of interesting, plausible, humorous, and intriguing ideas that may help us all learn the art of extreme relaxation. We may not have fully realized it yet, but we are on the verge of becoming desperate for a respite from the daily grind. I am constantly amazed at how audiences light up when I address them on the topic of extreme relaxation.

INFORMATION OVERLOAD: TMI

In my first book *The Trendmaster's Guide*, I shared a formula that was a ground rule in the Trend and Product Development office that I managed at Target:

$$TMI - E = TOXIC$$

Translated: Too much information without editing is toxic. In the book, I stated that "it's important to identify what's really important, and focus on just that." But that's hard to do these days. The ubiquity of technology in our lives has created a subculture of the Always On. The result is that we end up living in a virtual world, most of our time spent in front of a screen—the computer, the BlackBerry, the cell phone, the TV—and very little time spent actually dealing with the real world.

The result is a growing tension between productivity and freneticism. We are always busy, always on. We sit in meetings and surreptitiously use hand-held devices to exchange instant messages with someone in the same meeting. We check our BlackBerrys on the sidelines at our kids' soccer games. We attend social events but fail to turn off our cell phones. We watch TV, talk on the phone, and surf the net all in the same moment.

A recent Hewlett-Packard press release on the detrimental effects of "Info-Mania" pointed out that "an average worker's functioning IQ falls 10 points when distracted by ringing telephones and incoming e-mails . . . more than double the 4-point drop seen [in] studies on smoking marijuana."

OCD: Online Compulsive Disorder

The *New York Times* reported on a condition called OCD— online compulsive disorder—that manifests itself in people who are constantly wired into technology and just can't get enough data. For many, the lure of data, the ability to be constantly connected, is addictive. Some feel it's a small price to pay for survival in our competitive business environment. An edge, if you will.

BlackBerry once featured a paradoxical ad aimed at road

warriors; it read, "You're always out of your office. You're never out of your office." The smart business executive was shown on the run in an airport, communicating with his office in real time. That's great, but I wonder what the guy would have been doing if he was sitting on a lounge chair on a cruise ship. My guess? Probably the very same thing. Checking in with his office on his vacation time.

Experts at Harvard are studying the effects of online compulsive disorder. They are assessing how technology affects attention span, creativity, and focus. They believe that multitasking is not just annoying, but that it can be counterproductive and even addicting.

PSEUDO ATTENTION DEFICIT DISORDER

Psychologists trace a link between online compulsive disorder and another malady called pseudo attention deficit disorder, or PADD. While PADD sufferers don't actually have ADD (attention deficit disorder), the effects on the workplace and in their personal lives can be just as disruptive.

Workers addicted to data that have to be constantly "plugged in" tend to manifest the following conditions. First, their attention spans shorten, making it difficult for them to pay attention. They become frustrated with long-term projects and physically crave the bursts of stimulation that come from constantly checking their e-mails or phone messages. Some of the afflicted even find it difficult, if not impossible, to deal with downtime or quiet moments. And that's when personal relationships really begin to suffer.

We multitask to a ridiculous degree just to keep up, and we will eventually pay the price. We may gain something short term in the efficiency column, but what are we losing in the long run in the health and well-being column? More than one hundred years ago, Robert Louis Stevenson observed, "Extreme busyness is a sign of deficient vitality." My theory is that all that "extreme busyness" has to be offset by something that I call extreme relaxation.

CALL WOODS: Fight Fire with Fire

Businesses around the world are now searching for ways to help their workers "power unplug" throughout the day. The theory is that a deep-breath moment will help de-stress and re-balance the overworked workforce. If you can inject a little humor into the equation, so much the better.

Workers in Austria have access to a unique solution to all of this extreme busyness. Imagine you're having a bad day at work. Your numbers are down. Your systems are down. You are at your wit's end trying to concentrate and actually accomplish something, anything. You pick up your phone and dial into an automatic answering facility connected to cell phones hidden deep in the forests of southern Austria. It rings, and you are treated to a moment of . . . silence. The peaceful quiet you are listening to is disturbed only by the occasional thud of snow falling from a tree bough or by the footsteps of a deer passing by. You take a deep breath, and then hang up and go back to work, ready to focus again. The Call Woods project has proven to be so successful that a Call Waterfall and Call Mountaintop are planned.

THE HURRIED WOMAN SYNDROME

You've heard of the 4E's of executive performance that Jack Welch instituted while chairman and CEO of General Electric: energy, enthusiasm, execution, excellence. They're all great, but I've got a fifth E to add to the list: exhaustion.

Barriers between public and private, work and life have collapsed. At the same time that workers face increased pressures on the job, they are facing mounting responsibilities at home. Women in particular feel squeezed for time. Raising children, maintaining a household, caring for elders, sustaining personal relationships, planning for retirement, and, dare I mention it, finding a few hours a week to enjoy life, all end up being squeezed into our frantic schedules.

Dr. Brent W. Bost, author of the book *The Hurried Woman Syndrome,* reports that this "disease" affects 30 million women annually in the United States. HWS (also called predepression) is most commonly found in mothers who live with the chronic stress of trying to fulfill many roles for many people. It's characterized by a set of chronic physical, emotional, and psychological symptoms that include weight gain, moodiness, sleep problems, and low libido.

Another handle is what some experts now call multiminding. What is multiminding? Picture this: A typical woman, even if she appears to be relaxing in front of a late-night television show, reading a magazine, or tackling an array of projects at work, is actually constantly thinking about and preparing for the multiple dimensions of her life, mentally juggling an unending array of work, home, and self-care concerns while tackling or embracing the moment.

Studies conducted by Yahoo! and Starcom Media have led to what is being called the "38-hour day," where women indicate that their total time spent on individual activities in one day added up to thirty-eight hours of activity inside a twenty-four hour period. It's an extension of time compression, and it's leaving all of us with that much less time to wander the mall, watch TV, cook dinner, or spend time reading a long magazine or newspaper article. No wonder we're all exhausted, men and women alike!

PEACE OF MIND: One Moment at a Time

I received a Christmas card last year that exemplifies this concept in a humorous manner. It showed a glamorous but tired-looking woman (well coiffed but with dark circles under her eyes) reclining slightly and resting her head on her hand, a well-decorated Christmas tree in the background. The card read, "All she wanted for Christmas was a nap." When I show the card in my presentations, almost every woman in the audience either nods or sighs, practically in unison. The look in their eyes is one of complete "I've been there."

The same year I received that card, interestingly enough, Starbucks came out with a brilliant marketing campaign that announced, "The Holiday Drinks Are Here." The ad featured a large red cup of Starbucks coffee against a red background. The cup was front and center, and that's pretty much all you saw in the ad.

Except, you couldn't help but notice the white boxes along the side of the cup (featured front and center) that were used to indicate the customizable options:

Decaf/Deca'
Shots/Shots
Syrup/Sirop
Custom/Special
Drink/Boisson

In this case, however, there was a special box, right in the middle of all the options, checked with a thick black crayon that read:

One Moment to Myself

In essence, it was a celebration of a deep-breath moment, an acknowledgment that you are worth a small indulgence and a great indication of the fact that Starbucks understands the challenges the multiminded woman faces. They really get the fact that it's not just about the *coffee*, it's about the *experience*. In this case, One Moment to Myself is a precious gift to a hurried woman.

Marketers that help their customers embrace holistic approaches to a better way of living, help uncomplicate the complicated fabric of a woman's life today, and that can help show the way to extreme relaxation will have a big advantage when it comes to getting their attention, not to mention capturing their purchases.

IN BED: On the Road

With all of this busyness, you'd think we'd all be falling asleep at our desks or, at the very least, enjoying deep, albeit brief, nights' sleep. In reality, insomnia is on the rise worldwide as a result of our 24/7 culture, and bottom line, we are getting tired of being tired!

As a result, clever entrepreneurs in a variety of industries are devising offbeat ways to capitalize on our tiredness. The hotel industry is out in front on this trend. Westins offers Heavenly Beds to ensure that you get a good night's sleep while you're a guest at their hotels. The Four Seasons in Milan provides sleep CDs with music selected to help you fall asleep. The Lowry Hotel in Manchester, England, has a new Sleep Doctor service that helps you get the perfect night's sleep. Guests can order from a menu of sleep solutions ranging from different types of pillows to soothing spa treatments. Many hotels offer aromatherapy lines of bath salts and foaming bath oils with lavender that are thought to help induce sleep and relax the body and mind.

METRONAPS: Rest Easy

But what if you have, say, only twenty minutes to spare? Metro-Naps was born from the realization that many employees spend significant periods of their day dozing at their desks or catching power naps in odd places.

Founded in 2003 and researched and tested at Carnegie Mellon university, MetroNaps provides America with midday rest facilities: a clean, comfortable place to take a nap that is open to the public. The idea is to provide customers with the quick recharge they need so they can do more with their day, both professionally and personally.

The MetroPod is a womblike orb that uses ergonomics, white noise, ambient music, and audio-hypnosis to lull you into a relaxing twenty-minute power nap. The spalike sleep centers target office workers and road warrior travelers who need a serious break in their day. Their Web site welcomes you to the "future of workforce productivity," where a twenty-minute nap will cost about $14. Twenty minutes is the recommended length of sleep because anything longer would mean that you would have to be roused from deep REM sleep, and then you'd be in worse shape than before. Twenty minutes assures that you'll wake refreshed and ready to go again.

How does it work? First you check in at the nap center. You can call in advance, purchase a nap pass online, or just walk in. You recline in your pod and drift off as you listen to tranquil, relaxation-inducing music. The MetroNaps pod will wake you with a gentle combination of light and vibration after you've recharged. Next, you refresh. At the wake station, you utilize lotion, a facial spritz, and lemon-scented hand towels to help bring you back to the real world.

Gimmick or major technological advancement? Doctors and

research scientists agree that naps have been shown to benefit almost every aspect of human wellness. The benefits to the body include better heart functioning, hormonal maintenance, and cell repair. They help you live longer, stay more active, and look younger. A nap's positive effects on mental health include improved mood, lowered stress, and greater psychological balance. Wow! All that in twenty minutes or less? Yes, say the experts. Apparently benefits of naps can accrue in as little as five minutes. So there's an extreme relaxation concept that we can all embrace. Rest as an accessible treatment for everyone. After all, anyone can train him or herself to nap.

Interested? Want to give it a try? At this time, MetroNap daytime sleep salons are operated in the Empire State Building at 350 Fifth Avenue in New York, Suite 2410. And there's one coming soon to the Vancouver airport.

MALL NAPPING: Nap or Shop, It's Up to You!

I was surprised, but not overly so, when I discovered that a new nap concept opened up in my backyard in the Mall of America. In an article in the *Star Tribune*, staff writer Chris Serres reported that "the same mall that brought you a 74-foot Ferris wheel, a shark tank, and a children's dinosaur museum has leased 1,076 square feet of space to a company that charges 70 cents a minute for nap time." The new "store" is called MinneNAPolis. It is owned by a company called Power Nap Sleep Centers, Inc., of Boca Raton, Florida. There are three themed sleep rooms: Asian

Mist, Tropical Isle, and Deep Space. Each has its own unique ambience and design, and thick walls that guarantee to protect you from the kids screaming and squealing on the rides at the theme park down the shopping lane.

MinneNAPolis may likely become a prime refuge for husbands. They can power nap while their wives power shop. Most agree that it beats trying to sleep on the hard benches peppered throughout the public spaces in the mall.

BE PREPARED: What About Our Kids?

I wonder if we ever realize what we are modeling for our children. There's a saying that goes "Do as I say, not as I do." It's enlightening to take a look at what all of that OCD, HWS, and multiminding is forcing us to do to our kids. "Have my nanny call your nanny; we'll talk." Can't you just see a baby in diapers with a cell phone in hand making a comment like that? We're overscheduling our children's lives just as we are our own, squeezing playtimes for them around their music appreciation classes and swimming lessons.

GIRL SCOUTS OF AMERICA: REST ASSURED OR BE PREPARED?

Unfortunately, like mother, like daughter. Turns out that life at nine isn't always easy either. The peer pressure and packed schedules of our nation's youth have caused the Girl Scout Association of the USA to add a new badge to its modernized list of 166 badges that includes Car Care, Model Citizen, and Eco-Action. You earn this one by learning how to unwind.

The Stress Less badge for junior scouts aged eight to eleven is aimed at providing young girls with the resources and skills needed to cope with their own version of stress. The goal is to help them master relaxation techniques by pursuing such activities as breathing exercises, collecting favorite items in "stress kits," journal keeping, time management, and nature walks. More than sixty thousand young girls earned the badge the first year it was offered. What a great way to beat the stress of cookie-selling season!

SPA KIDS: TEEN TREATS

You might be surprised to learn that there are now day spas for kids. Virtually off-limits to kids only a few years ago, day spas are now welcoming stressed-out acne-assaulted children and their disposable incomes. Not that long ago, most spas wouldn't allow children under nineteen to come in. Now, many offer treatments and services specifically aimed at the pint-sized: Twinkle Toes pedicures, Fantasy Facials, and Yo Baby Yoga, to mention just a few. And here's a new summer camp idea. SPA Kids International now offers a program called S.P.A., also known as the Stress Proofing Adolescence program, that teaches teens stress-reduction techniques.

The travel industry has taken notice of our kids' yen for pampering too. Many high-end resort hotels are jazzing up their traditional amenities with more kid-friendly services. Carnival Cruise Lines offers a Generation Y kids spa on their cruise ships. The treatments are similar to the standards, but with a fun twist—for example, the fabulous fruity or acne attack facials. And budding young metrosexuals can sign up for a Surfer's Chest Wax—sure to attract the chicks.

The Tocasierra Spa, Salon, and Fitness at the Pointe Hilton Squaw Peak Resort in Phoenix offers a Princess for a Day package. For $70 and a 20 percent gratuity, girls get a manicure, pedicure, massage, and even a princess updo. The spa also offers Mommy and Me packages for mothers who want to be pampered along with their daughters. Turns out that 40 percent of spa-goers with children between the ages of thirteen and fifteen have taken their children to a spa.

AMERICAN GIRL SPA DOLL: I WANT TO BE JUST LIKE MOMMY

Back in the seventies, Barbie had her Corvette and Strawberry Shortcake had her strawberry-shaped dollhouse. In today's more enlightened times, the American Girl dolls have their very own spa. *Spa Finder* magazine reports "that the millions of girls aged 3 to 12 who collect American Girl dolls can now pamper them with amenities such as facial chairs, plush robes and slippers, and the popular Spa Treatment Kit, which includes a terry mitt, facial masks, cucumber slices, pretend nail polish, tiny flip-flops and toe nail decals." If you're lucky to find yourself in the vicinity of New York City's American Girl Place, you can even bring your doll in for an appointment to have her tresses professionally styled at the popular Doll Hair Salon.

Now that's what I call modeling for success.

THE SLOW FOOD MOVEMENT:
How to Hasten Slowly

Some people unwind at a spa, others may find nurture and cure for today's 24/7 world in the kitchen. The Slow Food Movement helps turn the kitchen into a haven for extreme relaxation. Slow Food is a nonprofit organization dedicated to preserving and supporting traditional ways of growing, producing, and preparing food. In other words, it is the countertrend to fast food.

Formed in 1989 in reaction to the opening of a McDonald's at the foot of Rome's beautiful Spanish Steps, the organization has grown steadily. Although it originated in Italy, it is spreading fast from hot spots in California and New York to points in between. There are now seventy chapters in forty states, some with more than one hundred members. Slow Food supports the concept of "hastening slowly." They acknowledge that many parts of our world have to be fast, but that we can choose to slow down, cook from scratch with fresh, old-fashioned heirloom natural ingredients, and take our time to enjoy a meal—one of the simple pleasures of life. Maybe we can't do it every night of the week, but we can make a conscious choice if we care enough about our health and well being.

Some of the most popular new cookbooks are enlightening chefs on this concept of "hastening slowly." *Slow Food: The Case for Taste* by Carlo Petrini; *The Slow Mediterranean Kitchen: Recipes for the Passionate Cook* by Paula Wolfort; and Corby Kummers 2001 award winner *The Pleasures of Slow Food: Celebrating Authentic Traditions, Flavors, and Tastes* are just three examples of cookbooks that promote slow food.

Erich Schlosser, author of *Fast Food Nation*, comments that "the Slow Food Movement stands in direct opposition to everything that a fast-food meal represents: blandness, uniformity, conformity, the blind worship of science and technology." Slow food is meant to be everything that fast food is not. It's slow—in the making and the eating. It's fresh—not processed. It's artisan ingredients from neighborhood farms and stores—not from industrial growers and retail Goliaths.

Perhaps it's time to enjoy food again the old-fashioned way—*slowly.*

THE GROOM ROOM: Haute Massage

If the spa or the kitchen doesn't help you relax in an extreme manner, then maybe a Groom Room is more up your alley. *Wallpaper* magazine offered up the idea of a Groom Room as the perfect way to end another stressful day; your own private space dedicated solely to taking care of yourself. A growing number of chic Brits have converted their extra bedrooms into their own "Groom Room, a private gym-cum-yoga-cum-beauty parlor."

According to the magazine, the Groom Room is "rapidly becoming the most important space in the house."

Here in the United States our leading luxury home building company, Toll Brothers, is installing meditation rooms in many of its new homes. The rooms feature aromatherapy storage and space for a massage table and yoga mats, and are complete with piped in nature sounds.

Some of these wellness spaces even feature movie theaters (with plasma flat screen, of course). Others showcase the latest in high-end workout equipment from Technogym (Technogym is to workout equipment what Bang & Olufsen is to home audio) or include the latest Bose stereo system, a massage table, and even self-contained showers and custom saunas and steam rooms. Many complete the space with a wet bar well stocked with nutra-ceuticals and designer waters.

The Groom Room is the perfect place to park your Gucci yoga mat, your Philippe Starck dumbbells, or your Everlast punching bag. It's also the latest one-upmanship point in conversations. The Groom Room has become the latest status symbol; being able to say that your masseuse is coming to your private relaxation chamber tops membership in the most elite club in London.

AERO BOLIVIA: Low and Slow

Today's world travelers love being able to get just about anywhere in the world on short notice. In many cases, whatever airline can get you where you're going fastest and cheapest is the preferred carrier. But there is an interesting countertrend that has developed in the vacation and travel industry. Bolivia's national airline, AeroSur, has unveiled a new kind of flying experience that's not about speed and convenience. They've refurbished big-window, thirty-seater Douglas DC-3 Dakotas that fly low and slow, and they've staffed them with flight attendants decked out in uniforms from the fifties.

The fifties'-style flights are just the ticket for older wealthy tourists looking for a taste of bygone days, as well as a close-up view of the scenery down below. Turns out they have the time to enjoy a leisurely flight experience and are happy to pay more for an engaging travel adventure. The scenery is magnificent, rugged and pristine. The wildlife is varied and abundant. And the low-flying planes allow you to savor the experience as well as photograph the memories. AeroSur offers twice-weekly ecotourism flights from LaPaz to Uyuni on its prop planes.

Hmmm. There's an interesting value proposition. Pay more to fly slower on older planes. A paradox to be sure, until you actually experience the adventure.

PLANNED SPONTANEITY:
Off the Cuff, On the Go

Some OCD-types need a different kind of getaway, farther from their kitchen, spa, or groom room. They really need to get away. The problem is, they don't have time to make elaborate plans and micromanage details. Their idea of getting away is to *plan* to have an *unplanned* getaway. An oxymoron, you say? Not according to Trendwatching.com.

They've dubbed this trend of acting on a whim, "planned

spontaneity." The term refers to the fact that booking a destination at the last minute has never been so easy. Making spontaneous decisions to go somewhere or do something is the
countertrend to our overplanned overscheduled lives. Trend-
watching.com comments, "Thanks to low fare regional airlines
that are popping up faster than you can say, 'obsolete national
carriers' booking on a whim has never been easier." You can book
roundtrip flights on easyJet and Ryanair in two minutes on the
Internet for as little as $20. Air Arabia is following suit. It's the
first Arab airline to focus on online booking and value for
money.

Studies show that almost 60 percent of travelers book their
flights within three days of traveling, and more than 20 percent
book just one day in advance. Now, a new hotel concept called
easyDorm can help you take care of the next leg of your last-
minute trip—your accommodations. No frills prefabricated
rooms are offered at ridiculously cheap rates, making spontaneous getaways even easier to plan. Or, opt for an easyCruise. Unlike traditional cruises, passengers can jump on and off the ship
as they desire and can also avoid huge dinners with the captain
by purchasing food from on-board concession stands.

If you know you've got a tough week ahead, you can decide to
plan to be spontaneous on Friday morning by determining when
and where you'll escape to that afternoon. Here today, gone tomorrow. Making spontaneous decisions to go somewhere is becoming the norm, especially for the Internet generation who does
everything at Internet speed.

SABBATICALS: Time for a Time-out?

American Demographics featured an article titled: "TIME OUT: More Americans want a break—from school, careers, marriages, even long-term commitments. The decision to take time off may not always be voluntary, but for many people, getting off the treadmill seems like the best way to stay on track."

I find that a most interesting paradox, and one that I can relate to very personally. For many, a sabbatical would be the ultimate getaway. It's long been one of the coveted privileges of tenured professors, but now the concept is extending beyond academia into the business mainstream. The article noted that in an ironic twist of fate, "propelled by today's economic climate, more companies are offering semi-paid 'leaves of absence' as an alternative to laying off employees."

While most Americans now work longer and longer hours at their jobs and put off retirement further and further down the road, some are countering that trend by making time to take a time-out. The trend has many contributing factors, starting with burnouts and layoffs to the constant effects of dealing with a world awash in terrorism. For many, post 9/11, values rearranged themselves and enjoying today became as important as planning for tomorrow.

Boy, talk about a silver lining! The dot-com bust, increased outsourcing, and globalization have all contributed to major layoffs in the economy. Those who were left with jobs worked that much harder to keep them, often doing the work of two people.

Many who were laid off had the opportunity to reevaluate their priorities.

When I left Target in November 2002, I took a six-month sabbatical to reassess what I wanted to do with the second half of my life. After thirty years in the retail business, endless twelve- and fourteen-hour days, and hundreds of thousands of air miles logged on the job, I was burned out and needed a break. My time off became an opportunity for inner growth, self-discovery, soul searching, and reinvention.

In 2001, the consumer research company Yankelovich reported on what they called "the marriage sabbatical." A marriage sabbatical is a planned time-out where spouses are allowed to take a predetermined amount of time away from each other to find themselves again. The idea is that if you know who you are and are happy with yourself, you are not only a better person, you become a better spouse. The Yankelovich report cited a survey that showed that a majority of married moms said "they needed to know themselves better," but that they don't have enough time to spend by themselves or on themselves.

Businesses may not have caught up with the desire to take sabbaticals (it's still a relatively small number of companies that offer them), but that shouldn't keep you from planning one for yourself. Taking a time-out may be the best thing you ever did for your career and your personal life. Smart companies will eventually realize that giving employees a hiatus can be extremely positive. Some already have. Workers come back with a renewed sense of focus and enthusiasm for their work and feel ready to take on the world.

Until then, if you are ready for a reinvention or a new adventure, why not work with a financial planner to figure out how you can give yourself the opportunity to get ahead by dropping out . . . temporarily?

LAUGHTER YOGA: Ha-Ha Health

By now I hope I've convinced you that the stress that is a part of all of our lives is no laughing matter. Or is it? Perhaps you've heard about laughter yoga. Maybe not, as most Americans have never heard of it, despite its worldwide popularity. It started with five people in 1995 and has grown into a worldwide movement with more than twenty-five hundred clubs in countries that include India, Canada, Dubai, Vietnam, Finland, Ireland, the United Kingdom, Australia, the United States, and many, many more.

The idea of laughter yoga was developed by Dr. Madan Kataria—a physician from Mumbai, India—who observed that anyone can laugh for fifteen to twenty minutes even if they don't have a good sense of humor, haven't heard a good joke in years, or just witnessed something funny. It combines laughter exercises (simulated laughter) and yoga breathing, which turn into real laughter when practiced in a group.

Why bother? Laughter yoga reportedly strengthens the immune system, unwinds the negative effects of stress, relieves

Laughter yoga in Denmark

anxiety, alleviates high blood pressure and asthma, increases pain tolerance, and is a powerful antidote for depression. It's also been shown to improve one's sense of humor, elevate self-confidence, and improve communication skills.

All that with a good belly laugh? Well, actually yes. *Worthwhile* magazine, in an article titled "Ha-Ha Laughter," reported that "Dr. Norman Cousins found in his groundbreaking 1964 studies that 10 minutes of laughter gave chronically suffering patients two hours of pain-free sleep, even without morphine." The Laughter Yoga Web site says that laughter is a teachable skill. We are all born with the capacity to laugh three hundred to four hundred times in a day, but unfortunately, we lose it in the process of growing up. By the time we reach age thirty-five, we are left with an average of just fifteen laughs a day.

Laughter yoga purports that you can laugh even if you are not happy, and that you should "fake it until you make it." Apparently you *can* fool Mother Nature. Our bodies can't tell pretend laughing from the real thing. The same set of happy chemicals is released whether laughter is real or self-induced. Part of the theory behind Laughter Clubs is that when you do it in a group, just watching the others fake the laughing is enough to get you really laughing.

In India, nearly five thousand people gather at laughter yoga events—on a regular basis, no less. Practitioners and gurus here in the United States predict that eventually, the corporate world will embrace it. Laughter is a powerful way to escape the cares and woes of the world, to lift our spirits, and it's catching on fast.

A good laugh just may be the last laugh when it comes to extreme relaxation.

In Praise of Slowness: How a Worldwide Movement Is Challenging the Cult of Speed is a great read that helps put the idea of extreme relaxation into context. Written by Carl Honore, the book highlights the history of our increasingly crazed relationship with time, or more specifically, our lack of it. Honore documents some amazing statistics: The average American spends seventy-two minutes of every day behind the wheel of a car; a typical business executive loses sixty-eight hours a year to being put on "hold"; and American adults currently devote, on average, a meager half

184 THE HUMMER AND THE MINI

hour per week to making love. Sounds pretty sad and empty, doesn't it?

No wonder we feel that we are living on the edge of exhaustion. Finally, we are beginning to admit to ourselves that things are out of control and that it's time to do something about it. Honore suggests that "slow is the new fast" and that a slow revolution is taking place. His "slow" philosophy can be summed up in a single word—*balance*. He notes, "People are discovering energy and efficiency where we may have least expected—in slowing down."

If this sounds a little desperate or hopeless, take heart. New avenues to de-stressing are popping up everywhere. People are flocking to yoga, practicing meditation, and spending as much time at their local spa as they did a few years ago at the gym. They are traveling to the ends of the earth, literally, for a life-changing rejuvenating vacation. They have even found a way to chant with Deepak Chopra on their cell phones. You can now give yourself a Zap of Zen on your cell phone plan. For $3.95 a month, Sprint and Verizon Wireless users can receive enlightening quotes, inspirational images, and Deepak's weekly messages.

Someday, someone will offer an *ommmm* ring tone for the cell phone. Just about anything goes when it comes to creative versions of extreme relaxation.

CONCLUSION

Inner peace? Who has time? You do, if you get creative with extreme relaxation.

The emerging trend in business is the sixty-hour workweek: traveling 40 percent of the time, cell phones and pagers always on. The wise employers and savvy marketers are those who can identify the countertrend—which is, in essence, recognizing our growing need to decompress.

CHAPTER 9
SOCIAL CAPITALISM

IS IT POSSIBLE TO MAKE MONEY AND DO GOOD AT THE SAME time? Our corporate world is rooted in capitalism—the bottom line rules. So it follows that the business of making money tends to far outweigh the ideal of doing good. In the last few years, we've seen the corporate world rocked by personal greed and great scandal. While things are beginning to change, we still have a long way to go before "greed is good" is supplanted by "doing good." It's nice to think that, eventually, doing good and making money will be considered business as usual.

Every era has had their robber barons. Because of the contributions they have brought to society (for example, railroads, factories, libraries, and museums), their greed has oftentimes been overlooked, or at least minimized with the telling of history. The irony today is that many of these new social capital leaders aren't just embracing new business policies out of the goodness of their hearts. They are doing it to make money. The difference is that they are consciously choosing a different way to do business, making decisions based on different prerequisites, in order to do good *first*, and then ultimately making more money.

GREED IS GOOD:
How Much Is Enough CEO Pay?

In the business world, the "greed is good" mantra still seems to be in full force. Just take a look at CEO pay. On Labor Day 2005, the *New York Times* reported that according to the Institute for Policy Studies and United for a Fair Economy, the ratio of the average chief executive's pay to that of production workers smashed through the four hundred to one barrier. That is to say, for every $1 earned by the average worker, the boss earned $431.

Just a few years before, the ratio was two hundred to one. To give you a better perspective on the out-of-whack situation, look at it this way: If the minimum wage had kept pace with CEO pay since 1990, the minimum wage would be $23.03 an hour. Obviously, we're a long way from that scenario. The good news is that some boards (nudged by investors) are ahead of the trend curve and have begun to ask the question "How much CEO pay is enough?"

ETHICAL CONSUMPTION:
Doing Good by Shopping Well

We've seen other ethical "do good" issues surface repeatedly as well. The environment, health, and fair trade practices have become major consumer hot buttons. For instance, the backlash against SUVs and their exorbitant fuel consumption (the What Would Jesus Drive? campaign) made a huge impact on the automobile industry even before the price of gas hit $3 a gallon. Nike and Gap have been battered by fair trade issues and, as a result, have instituted many new highly visible and transparent policies for production in third-world countries. On another level, McDonald's was practically shamed into offering salads on their menu and removing the Big Gulp from their drink lineup by media attention on the child obesity epidemic and the fallout from the movie *Super Size Me*.

Today, even the strongest of mainstream brands know they can be irrevocably hurt by reports of unethical practices. Many have learned the hard way that strong branding will take you only so far and that they can no longer rely on their logo alone to combat negative reports and alleviate consumers' concerns.

ETHICAL SHOPPING: Eccentric or Savvy?

Anita Roddick of the Body Shop, Horst Reckelbacher of Aveda, and Roxanne Quimby of Burt's Bees were pioneers of the "do good, make money" philosophy. They were, for all practical purposes, practicing the principles of social capitalism before anyone was reporting on it. Back then, in the early eighties, cosmetic manufacturers that subscribed to natural and environmental practices and practiced socially responsible development and procurement were considered "eccentric herbalist hippies."

Today those eccentric herbalist hippies are setting the standard. Now they are considered "savvy business marketers." Environmentally friendly beauty products are throwing off their unglamorous socks-and-sandals image. Eco is fast becoming the label of the future of luxury cosmetics.

Over the past few decades, there has been growing public interest in the ethical implications of consumption. Whether the concerns are political, ecological, or socioeconomic, all are ethical in the sense that they are concerned with the "right way" for a group or company to conduct itself in society.

A report on ethical consumption on WGSN (Worth Global Style Network) summed up the reason for this sea change as follows: "The rise of consumerism during the 20th century saw brands become increasingly powerful social and economic forces. Companies like Nike, Disney, and Ford were not seen just as producers or suppliers but as symbols of entrepreneurship, fashion, innovation, wealth, or success."

Toward the end of the century, things began to change. Consumers increasingly started associating these companies with corporate greed and injustice, as opposed to seeing them as aspirational lifestyle brands. Although criticism of large organizations was nothing new, it had never before been such an everyday part of consumers' lives.

Socially conscious consumers are now voting with their pocketbooks. According to Henley World research, in the last year, in some countries, up to 70 percent of people have stopped buying products for ethical or environmental reasons. The commercial impact of ethical consumption has increased considerably in the last few years. Whether the concerns are political, ecological, or socioeconomic, all are ethical in the sense that they are concerned with the "right way" for groups or companies to conduct their business in society.

SOCIAL RESPONSIBILITY:
Doing Good Is Good for Business

Today's progressive companies are finding new ways of doing business that have as much to do with doing good as they do with making money. Some of America's most visionary leaders have come to believe that the best way to make money just might have something to do with saving the world.

Today's advocates of corporate social responsibility want to do good *and* make money. Visionary leaders such as James Sinegal at Costco, Howard Schultz of Starbucks, and Paul Dolan of Fetzer Vineyards are building a different kind of company, one that marries profit and purpose. They all believe that socially responsible companies will eventually outperform their competitors and their peers. But it's important to realize that it's not *just* about conscience. It's still about making money.

These companies are boldly challenging the long-held assumptions that the only way to increase profits is to squeeze every last dollar out of your costs, pay your employees as little as possible, and engage in ruthless cutthroat competition. Instead, they've developed enlightened policies that treat workers with dignity and respect, thereby reenergizing their workforces, im-

proving morale, and lowering turnover costs significantly. Practices such as these ultimately result in a stellar reputation with
investors and consumers that will pay off at the bottom line. In
other words, they are showing the world that doing good is good
for business.

WORTHWHILE MAGAZINE:
Purpose, Passion, and Profit

There's even a new business magazine dedicated to the concept of
ethical business. It's called *Worthwhile* and is described by some
as a cross between *Fast Company, Oprah,* and *Vanity Fair.* Their
editorial mission is to put purpose and passion on the same plain
as profit. *Worthwhile* offers a roadmap for business success that is
more personally fulfilling and socially responsible. Created by
Anita Sharpe and Kevin Salwen, both veterans of the *Wall Street
Journal,* their magazine's motto is that it is impossible to have a
meaningful life without meaningful work.

Determined to put a little soul and passion back into the
workplace, the founding editors both acknowledge that the old
contract that companies once had with their employees is long
gone, a victim of corporate layoffs, downsizing, outsourcing, Six
Sigma, and globalization. They maintain that if you're looking
for a heart and soul connection at work, don't count on your em-
ployer. Smart companies and enterprising individuals need to
empower themselves and find a new way to do business; and
Worthwhile aims to help them to do just that.

A few years ago, a magazine based on this premise would

have been written off in the business world as too "touchy feely." And there probably wouldn't have been enough of the right kind of stories to fill the pages. But the time appears to be right for a new approach to looking at the corporate world. As Salwen says, "Business magazines are all aimed at the brain. This will be the first business magazine focused on the heart and the soul."

That not only sounds good, it feels great and sells magazines too.

THE GOOD CEO: Not an Oxymoron

A few years back, *BusinessWeek* magazine did a cover story titled "The Good CEO." Shopkeepers, coffee makers, peddlers of beauty creams, distillers of spirits, and even chefs can all fit the description of "good CEOs." Here's my all-star lineup.

PAUL DOLAN: FERMENTING A BUSINESS REVOLUTION

Paul Dolan, president of Fetzer Vineyards, is also the author of *True to Our Roots: Fermenting a Business Revolution.* He's a fourth-generation winemaker who was converted ahead of the curve to organic farming methods. His revolution has as much to do with the environment and taking good care of employees as it does with a profitable bottom line.

In his book, Dolan urges all businesses to commit to what he calls "the triple bottom line," or E3. Every decision at his company is put to the E3 test. The three Es stand for:

1. ECONOMICS: Does it make economic sense? Can we make money?
2. ENVIRONMENT: Does it protect or improve the environment?
3. EQUITY: Does it support fair and safe standards for all employees?

In his words, "No margin, no mission." In a competitive business such as winemaking, you won't last long if you can't make money. He's instituted measures such as converting his entire fleet of tractors to bio-diesel fuel, providing housing on the grounds for the migrant workers, funding vaccines for preventative immunizations for their children, and providing English language lessons to his workers, most of whom are from Mexico and don't speak the language well when they arrive.

As it turns out, all of those sustainable business practices are paying off at the bottom line, and the message is spreading to other businesses and corporations, even those not in the wine business. As *Fast Company* reported in an article entitled "The Good Earth," "It's an intoxicating idea: Good environmental and social practices blend nicely with sound business."

I'll drink to that.

AMAZON RAINFOREST VODKA: SWEET SUCCESS

And so will Thomas Cleaver, president and founder of Amazon Vodka. His Rainforest Vodka is one of the most unusual vodkas ever imported into the United States. It's made in Brazil with a special sugar-cane recipe that delivers a sweet and ultrasmooth taste compared to other harsh grain or potato-based vodkas. It's double distilled with a special process that gives it a clean and crisp finish.

Every bottle of Amazon Rainforest vodka (priced around $23.50) comes with a special gift with purchase. Each bottle comes with a preservation deed for five thousand square feet of pristine rain forest from the Rainforest Preservation Foundation of South America. The foundation places the land into a perpetual trust, with a guarantee that it will never be sold or destroyed. You might think it's just another marketing gimmick. But when you realize that 108,000 acres of rain forest disappear each day, 75 acres a minute, you have to commend a company for trying to reverse the trend and put a finger in the dike of sustainability.

As Cleaver notes, there are more than 22 million environmentalists and younger people who haven't yet chosen their preferred vodka. They may still be in the beer and wine stages. But when they're ready to move up to mixed drinks, he wants to give them a better reason to select his vodka over Belvedere or Grey Goose.

It sounds like a sweet deal to me.

COSTCO: THE RESPECTFUL REBEL

James Sinegal thumbs his nose (respectfully) at Wall Street when analysts admonish him for paying high salaries and offering incredibly low prices. Often criticized for his generous pay and benefit policies, he stubbornly refuses to change his success formula to suit Wall Street's old-fashioned demands.

Here are some numbers that may surprise you. At Costco, the average pay is around $17 hour, compared to a little over $11 hour at Sam's Club. The health plan is one of the best in the retail business, and the company contributes generously to its workers' 401(k) plans. In contrast to other CEOs, Sinegal caps his salary at approximately three times what his highest-paid store managers make, and many of them make more than six figures. As an example, his salary for 2004 was just $350,000, which puts his at less than 10 percent of many other chief executives' paychecks. Many years in the past, he's turned down bonuses from the board as well. The *New York Times* has quoted him as saying, "I've been very well rewarded. If you're going to try and run an organization that's very cost-conscious, you can't have those disparities. Having an individual making 100 or 200 (never mind 400!) times more than the average person working on the floor is wrong." In many ways, Mr. Sinegal sets a good example of how to succeed in business by doing the right thing.

His cardinal rule is that no branded item should ever be marked up by more than 14 percent, and no private label item by more than 15 percent. (As a frame of reference, most supermarkets mark up their goods in the neighborhood of 25 percent, and department stores by 50 percent or more.) But for many customers, it's not just about price, it's more about the treasure hunt. You can buy anything from Waterford crystal to ahi tuna, diamond rings to peanut butter, pinpoint oxford shirts to printer ink, Dom Perignon champagne to motor oil, coffins to infant formula, all with a trip to Costco.

Shortsighted analysts continue to suggest that Sinegal should take better care of the shareholders. But he stubbornly refuses to cut benefits or employee pay, and responds by saying that by taking care of his employees, he will be taking better care of his customers, and that will ultimately take good care of the shareholders. Costco is the undisputed leader in the $75 billion warehouse club business. They've captured a 50 percent share of the market, and their warehouse stores generate sales per square foot double that of Sam's Club.

Turns out nice guys can finish first after all.

BEST BUY: BEST CEO

Another good CEO, in my book is Brad Anderson of Best Buy. The consumer-electronics retailing giant had sales of more than $27.5 billion for the fiscal year 2004, more than double their sales of just five years before. Research firm Retail Forward puts their sales per square foot at $870, in contrast to Circuit City's $480 per square foot.

Anderson has instituted many groundbreaking and forward-thinking business strategies and practices at Best Buy, considered one of the most consumer-centric companies in retailing. The organization leverages in-depth research that segments their customers and stores into specific targeted profiles and then carefully designs and markets to them. For instance, Best Buy acquired the Geek Squad in 2002, in part to help service the customer better after purchase, but also to help dazed and confused shoppers with their initial selections. It's that kind of vision that's been driving sales aggressively and trouncing the competition along the way.

But Anderson exhibits another kind of insight and generosity that is rare among leaders today. Linda Tischler, of *Fast Company*, calls this new breed of leaders Aquarian CEOs. These CEOs are, as she puts it "farsighted, tolerant, humane and practical. And they have the courage of their convictions, even when it means staring down myopic criticism from Wall Street." Theirs is a club where the highest ethical standards rank as the price of admission, and vision and common sense are as important as strategy and execution.

Anderson walks that talk beautifully. It's not well known among the general public, or even within the business community at large, but a few years ago, the CEO made a historic decision regarding his annual pay. In 2003, he earned $3.2 million in pay (base salary plus bonus), but he turned down another key part of his compensation. The board granted him two hundred thousand stock options worth more than $7.5 million at the time. Instead of pocketing the additional pay, he *gave away the options* to nonexecutive hourly workers directly involved with the customer on the floor, day in and day out.

Imagine turning down $7.5 million because you "have enough"! Truthfully, I *can't* imagine why stories like these don't

198 THE HUMMER AND THE MINI

make the headline news. We need to hear that these kinds of stories are out there in the greed-obsessed world of Enron, Tyco, and World Com.

Kudos to Mr. Anderson for realizing that the success of a retailing company doesn't emanate down from the executive floor but up from the sales floor.

HOWARD SHULTZ: BENEVOLENT BREWER

Howard Schultz, founder of Starbucks, is also a huge believer in being socially conscious. He has said from the first cup of coffee that he "prefers to make a profit in a benevolent manner." Now that's what I call a great platform for a business plan.

He believes that consumers will perform their own cultural audits when they have a choice between X and Y. If two products are essentially the same, customers will eventually begin to ask more serious questions. What does the company stand for? How do they treat the people who work for them? And do they give back to the community?

During the 2005 holiday season, Starbucks ran a full-page ad in the *New York Times* to show their customers that they can put their money where their mouth is. The ad said the following:

Who needs a coffee machine?

Maybe we should think of companies less like machines and more like individuals? With a machine, you just turn it on and it does its job. It has no responsibilities and no morals. And it has no future. An individual—

and a corporation—is obligated to live in the world according to human principles in the present, or else it cannot thrive in the future. For us, this means remembering that we are more than a coffee company; we are a people company, serving coffee one person at a time.

To learn more about what we hold dear, visit: www.starbucks.com/goodbusiness

Schultz set out to build a different kind of company—a company that had a conscience. He succeeded in beans. He managed to achieve a healthy balance of profitability, shareholder value, a sense of benevolence, and a social conscience.

JAMIE OLIVER: COOKING WITH PASSION

If you watch the Food Network, chances are you know who Jamie Oliver is. Better known as The Naked Chef, he's one of the new genre of Celebrity Chefs. The young Brit is phenomenally successful. He stars in two television cooking shows and is the author of several best-selling cookbooks that have sold more than eight million copies around the world.

His first project was Fifteen, a big ticket—but nonprofit—restaurant partially staffed by displaced and disadvantaged young people that he literally rescues from a life on the street. It's called Fifteen because the project started out with fifteen unemployed kids. In addition to being unemployed when they were recruited, many were homeless and some had learning difficulties. Participants spent a year under Oliver's tutelage, learning all aspects of the restaurant trade, before they moved on to high-paying jobs in the field.

The program is in its fifth year, and a second Fifteen restaurant just opened in Amsterdam in 2006. All proceeds from both restaurants go to the Fifteen Foundation (the charity formerly known as Cheeky Chops). Fifteen has gotten great reviews and is perpetually booked, often weeks in advance. Jamie doesn't make a dime from the venture. His return is inspiring young kids and developing new talent.

Jamie's most recent socially conscious venture is the Feed Me Better campaign designed to raise culinary taste levels and healthy-eating standards for schoolkids in the United Kingdom. The campaign, headed by Jamie, was highlighted in a 2005 TV program in Britain called *Jamie's School Dinners*. For the series, Jamie basically took charge of a London borough that serves twenty thousand school meals a day. The public was outraged to discover that as little as 39 pence (65 cents) is the average cost per child currently spent on school lunches. The food is often processed, repetitive, and severely lacking in nutrition. Jamie's goal is to put tasty and, above all, nutritious food back on the school menus.

After the TV show initially ran, a petition was circulated requesting that the government allocate more money to feed the children better, and it was delivered to Tony Blair at 10 Downing Street. As a result, the government promised to spend £280 million to improve school lunches across the country.

The Feed Me Better campaign is Jamie's way of educating others and sharing the fruits of his labor. As he says on the campaign's Web site, "Being a good cook isn't about being born to it, it's about discovery and growth."

Sounds like a good recipe for a successful life to me.

SOUL AND BUSINESS:
Not Mutually Exclusive Anymore

I know I'm not alone in thinking that it's time to put a little soul back into the $. It doesn't matter whether you run a hotel or a country, there is a better way to work and live than many of us have experienced in corporate America. Here are two final stories, about as far apart in magnitude as you can get, that are managing to put a little more spirit and soul into the workplace and the world.

DAKLOOS: DUTCH TREAT

Have you ever traveled to an unknown city and not known where you were going to stay because all the hotels are full, and as it got later and later you were afraid you might end up on the street? Well, that may be as close as you've ever come to feeling homeless. But to many who actually live on the streets, that feeling is one they experience every day.

Dakloos is the Dutch word for "homeless." It's also the name of an innovative accommodation-booking Web site dedicated to eradicating homelessness in the Netherlands and around the world. The www.dakloos.nl site is linked to a very large online hotel data bank that has thousands of participating hotels offering discounted rates and special packages. Customers get low Internet rates, and Dakloos donates 3 percent of revenues to the homeless in Amsterdam.

In other words, you get a professional, reliable, quick-and-easy method to book your reservations and the best prices available. You won't pay a penny extra for your hotel accommodation. Hotels such as Le Meridien, Sheraton, Starwood, Golden Tulip, Sofitel, Hilton, Holiday Inn, and more are all participating. Bottom line, they fill their rooms, you spend your night in a fashionable hotel, and some unknown soul spends a night off the street.

Sounds like a good nights' sleep for all.

SPIRIT IN BUSINESS: An Oxymoron?

Mixing spirit and business isn't a complete oxymoron. Spirit in Business doesn't think so, anyway. Founded in April 2002 as a global community of leaders and businesses, Spirit in Business explores ways to effectively lead our organizations to higher performance in order to benefit stakeholders and society as a whole at the same time. It's an organization that helps identify companies with leaders who are purposeful, passionate, and principled in their endeavors. Their goal is to help create a world and an economy that works for everyone. They envision a world that is more beautiful, an economy that is more equitable, and a society that is more creative. To achieve that end, they sponsored the International Conference on Gross National Happiness.

Sound strange? It seems that one of the complexities of showing the corporate world the energy and opportunity that can result from nurturing the spirit in their teams and their organizations is that it's almost impossible to offer a measurement-prone capitalist society something as apparently unmeasurable as "happiness."

Thanks to a visionary leader, there is a striking example of how to rethink how progress is measured. We just need to think about measuring national prosperity with an index different from that of the usual Gross Domestic Production (GDP) index. The GDP is a purely economic statistic. It tallies up the value of all goods and services that are exchanged for money. The more goods bought and sold, no matter what those goods are or even if they are good for you, the higher the GDP, which is supposed to be an indicator of the country's general well being. The irony is that if you stop to *really* think about it, the things that truly make us happy—good health, a clean environment, a caring community, and stable families—count for nothing in the GDP.

While Western economies struggle to grow and face the consequences of the ongoing drive for more, more, more, a small Himalayan country the size of Switzerland is developing a way to measure progress with gross national *happiness* instead of gross national *product*. The king of Bhutan, Jigme Singye Wangchuck, is way ahead of the times. Thirty years ago, he declared, "Gross national happiness is more important than gross national product."

And he's putting his money where his beliefs are. Over the

years, Wangchuck has been working with a number of organizations and consultants to develop an alternative measurement index called the Gross Domestic Happiness (GDH) index. The goal of this new index is to give a more realistic and less intangible measure of what in the end should be the real goal of a nation—to improve the lives of its citizens.

In 1998, the Bhutan government unveiled the "four pillars of happiness" by which they would attempt to measure their citizens' happiness: sustainable economic development, conservation of the environment, promotion of national culture, and good governance. Together, these four pillars create conditions in which every individual will be able to pursue happiness with reasonable success.

Bhutan's success with the four pillars is remarkable. People in Bhutan speak of "the outside world" as if it were another celestial body. The rest of the Indian subcontinent is awash in corruption, ethnic struggle, illiteracy, pollution, poverty, and the clash of civilizations. Bhutan, with its emphasis on its citizens' happiness (as opposed to its production) stands out as a shining star of pacifism, paternalism, and egalitarianism.

Seems as though there may really be a "paradise on earth."

CONCLUSION

Bottom line (and that's where it ultimately counts), given the choice, most of us would prefer to make money and do good at the same time. In order to accomplish that goal in the future, more and more of us will consciously opt for goods that are ethically produced. We'll reevaluate the companies we choose to work for as well as buy from. We'll begin to emulate the good CEOs. We'll take care of the environment and our workers. And hopefully we'll begin to find ways to put some spirit and soul back into our work and our lives. That will be the ultimate payback.

Perhaps it's time to revisit the standard accounting methods and old measures of success that most businesses still use today, standards that don't seem to take into account the current valuation of what's *important* to customers today.

CHAPTER 10
THE PARADOX OF SUCCESS

THE ULTIMATE PARADOX IS WHAT I CALL THE PARADOX OF success. Put simply, the paradox of "the good life" is that we all appear to be living more frantic, less satisfactory lives, despite far greater affluence.

Study after study reports that once the basic human concerns of hunger and warmth have been addressed, we begin our quest for more, more, more. In order to attain more, we work harder, and as we work harder, we have less and less time with which to enjoy what we worked so hard to attain. Work and spend become a habit.

THE SCARCITY SHORTAGE

Seth Godin, author of *The Purple Cow*, believes that we are all becoming victims of what he calls a "scarcity shortage." In an article for *Fast Company*, he craftily warns us that we are running out of scarcity. Wait a minute. Isn't it *good* to have a lot of everything? Seth points out that perhaps we are all victims of too many things flooding the marketplace. That's why everything ends up looking alike. When there's too much of too many things that look a whole lot alike, it follows that everything becomes a little less valuable, and a lot less special.

THE HAPPINESS GAP

We are caught in what *Elle* magazine profiles as "the happiness gap." The happiness gap is a place between wanting (and getting) more, and never having enough. How can having more be a problem? British economist Richard Layard, in his book *Happiness: Lessons from the New Science of Emotional Well-Being*, examines a mountain of data and comes to the conclusion that we are all struggling with "the paradox at the heart of modern culture: As societies grow richer, they do not become happier."

If that is indeed true, why do we continue to want more, and why are we all working so hard? Scientists point to the "hedonic treadmill" as a perpetrator of our misery. We all have wants. Once those wants are addressed, they are no longer wants because they have been satisfied. We check them off our list, so to speak. But it's not that easy. It turns out that wanting more is a basic instinct. Inevitably, something else is waiting in the wings to be added to our want list. And the search for more continues. More stuff anyway, if not more meaning.

HOW MUCH IS ENOUGH?

It's difficult to get off that treadmill. In order to do so, we each need to ask ourselves a basic question: How much is enough? That's a question that more and more consumers are beginning to ask themselves. We are waking up to the idea that unhappiness is not knowing what we really want, and killing ourselves to get it.

Boomers, accustomed all their lives to feeling entitled to the good life, are asking themselves What exactly is "the good life" anyway? And what is "happiness?" Gen X and Y, seeing the unhappiness and destruction brought about by the previous generation's endless quest for more, are beginning to formulate new visions of what success, or the good life, means to them. They seem to be unwilling to sacrifice everything today in order to accumulate all of the things they once thought they needed tomorrow. They are reevaluating the value equation, and perhaps it's time that business does as well.

MARKETERS: Embrace the Paradox!

An old Finnish proverb states: "Happiness is a place between too little and too much." Most marketers, charged with the mission of selling "more stuff" to more people, might shudder at that thought. Rather than selling more stuff, what if you could help your customers find that place between too little and too much? What if you could help your customers embrace the ultimate paradox that that thought represents? What if less is, indeed, more?

AND. . . NOT EITHER/OR

Paradoxes make life interesting. Remembering what Charles Handy said, "Paradoxes are to be lived with, not solved," I believe you can discover new approaches to old problems by embracing the paradoxes. It's time we let go of the idea that the answers are black and white. I believe we need to consider an *and* approach to business, instead of an *either/or* approach. What would that mean? What would that look like? Very simply, it would mean that we look for:

- Scarcity as well as abundance
- The old remade into the new
- Commodities transformed into luxuries
- Customization for everyone
- Make-believe made real
- Indulgences that are good for you
- Less that really becomes more
- Extreme stress offset by extreme relaxation
- Doing good and making money
- Expense control and creativity

Remember the "Churning Ocean of Milk" at Angkor Wat? I believe that the way to keep our business environment from turning sour is to learn to live with the push and pull of opposites, to balance the contradictions and inconsistencies, and to embrace the paradoxes—the trends and countertrends—that exist at a macro level in our world. It's a great lesson. Life may be more complicated than we'd wish, but it's also simpler than we realize. We simply need to embrace the power of paradox and put it to work for us.

ACKNOWLEDGMENTS

KHALIL GIBRAN SAID, "THE OBVIOUS IS THAT WHICH IS never seen until someone expresses it simply." To me, that sums up what I believe to be the power of paradox. The power lies in the ability to take a thought that at first glance is unbelievable, unachievable, or impossible, and use the paradox to concisely illuminate the simple and succinct truth that lies at the core of that idea.

Most of the thoughts, lessons, musings, and examples in this book are secondhand learnings that I have accumulated by voraciously reading the works of others far smarter than I. When I first read David Brooks's book *Bobos in Paradise: The New Upper Class and How They Got There*, I became enchanted by the idea of paradox. His ideas were so beautifully captured in his witty prose that I launched myself into a decade long study of paradox.

I freely admit that my thoughts on paradox aren't new, nor are they revolutionary. Others have explored the world of paradox at great length, and I have learned much from them. I was particularly inspired by Charles Handy and his 1994 book, *The Age of Paradox*, an international best seller that helped me understand that paradoxes held possibilities, if not answers, to things that had been bothering me about the world of trend for quite some time. I hope that my interpretations of trend/countertrend have proven to be insightful to the reader.

Margaret Mead said, "Humans think in metaphors and learn through stories." I've tried to leverage that idea throughout the book by using the stories, data, and examples that I gleaned by reading endless magazine and newspaper articles written by others. I have tried to properly credit each tidbit and piece of trivia from my research that I've borrowed to help the reader discover the power of paradox. By telling the stories in my own way, I hope I've brought some unique insights to the equation and helped you reframe your way of looking at the world, or at the very least, the marketplace.

My first book, *The Trendmaster's Guide: Get a Jump on What Your Customer Wants Next*, was a simple and witty handbook of my personal philosophies on the *how* of trend. This book is meant to be a birds-eye view of *what* the trends are that are affecting the hearts and minds of the consumer. It was much harder to write than I thought it would be.

I would never have completed this work without the support and kindness of a great number of people along the way. Great good thanks and humble appreciation to Michael Spoodis, who helped me with the early editing and challenged my thinking and my writing. I would never have made my deadlines without you.

Karen Holseth-Broekema, if you hadn't offered to sublease your *casita* in San Miguel to me that March, I never would have gotten started. I am certain that the bougainvillea petals outside my door and my window added insights to my inspiration. George Lopuch, without your enthusiastic review of my introduction, I never would have gotten to Chapter 1.

Thanks also to Anne Berg, Nathan Dungan, and George Dow for your ideas, inspiration, and insights along the way. Helen Chargo, without your calming and encouraging words every time I got stuck, I never would have found a way to have a life *and* honor my obligation to my publisher.

Thank you to my publisher, Adrian Zackheim, for believing enough in the power of paradox to sign me up for a second book; to Jonathon Lazear, my agent, who recognized the power of paradox from the get-go; to Will Weisser for his constant support, to my copy editor, Debbie Weiss Gieline, and especially to Adrienne Schultz for her guidance and editing expertise.

Thanks also to my mom, Lorraine, for teaching me as a child about "having your cake and eating it too." We weren't supposed to be able to do that, but a funny thing happened on the way to becoming a Trendmaster.

Last, thanks to my husband, Gary, for his love and support and constant belief that what I was doing was important enough to work around. Thank you for holding me tight while letting me head off to pursue my dreams.

INDEX

CREDITS